CONTEMPORARY AMERICAN
INDIAN LEADERS

Contemporary American Indian Leaders

MARION E. GRIDLEY

ILLUSTRATED WITH PHOTOGRAPHS

DODD, MEAD & COMPANY

NEW YORK

7319335

ISBN: 0–396–06633–X
Library of Congress Catalog Card Number: 72–3148

Printed in the United States of America
by The Cornwall Press, Inc., Cornwall, N.Y.

To those many Indian people whose
friendships I have cherished

Contents

Introduction

American Indians, as a whole, do not have strong national leaders in the sense and to the degree that the black people do. To understand why this is so, one must go back into Indian history and culture.

For one thing, Indians are accustomed to think of themselves as tribal groups rather than as a national people. Nationalism is beginning to emerge but does not, as yet, have strong roots. Indian relations with the government vary and are on a tribal basis, and attempts at unity and concerted action have often been circumvented in the face of the tribal concept.

Such historic leaders as King Philip, Pontiac, and Tecumseh found the tribal concept the one great barricade to their plans for the formation of Indian confederations for the purpose of acting against the whites and driving them out. It was difficult to break down ancient enmities or to overcome long-standing jealousies in order to gain the needed strength of united effort. There were also situations where some tribes found it advantageous to side with the whites or to use the whites to fight their battles against stronger tribes. There were both economical and political benefits in such action.

From the time of the first meeting with the whites, Indian politics played a major role in the separation of the tribes, as much so as any undermining or subversion on the part of the white man. It is just as true that whites were able to capitalize and exploit Indian politics for their own ends.

In Indian culture, young men were held back from assuming the mantle of leadership. They could not express their views in council until they had gained stature as warriors. Leadership belonged to the tried and the experienced. A young person could, and must, however, aspire to be a leader, and all of his training was directed to that end. Only the very outstanding, such as Tecumseh, Crazy Horse, and Osceola, became leaders in their youth. The urgency of the time projected them to the fore.

Indian culture was based on a purely communal life. Although the tribes varied greatly in custom, language, and costume, according to the environment in which they lived, the share-and-share-alike philosophy was almost universal. The chiefs were not rulers, but dedicated to the welfare of their people. There was no ownership of property or land, which was a gift from the Great Spirit. Indians lived upon the land but also cared for the land.

While territorial boundaries were recognized, these were protective of hunting rather than designating land ownership. Land was never intended to get rich on, and it could not be sold or traded. There were rules which regulated hunting and warfare, but there were no laws, and neither were there locks and keys.

With an entirely different approach to life stemming from a civilization based on materialism, the divine right of kings, and the intricacies of law, the white settlers surrounded the Indian communities and made little islands of them. They also imposed their own images upon the Indians, who had little or no understanding of what that image was, yet were expected to conform to it.

When protest set in, each tribe acted for itself, and lost. It was soon too late for Indian leadership, in a united effort, to assert itself. And so King Philip, Pontiac, Tecumseh, and the rest went down to tragic defeat.

Once Indians were culturally and economically shattered, there was no way for them to exist except as dependents on the "mercy" and "generosity" of the "Great White Father" and his benevolence was many times neither merciful or generous.

After the establishment of the various reservations, an attempt was made to guide Indians on "a new trail," to make of them farmers, to educate them for trades and as domestics, and to use them as the "bell sheep" who would help recruit others to follow in their footsteps as "simulated" whites. (The reservation policy was established in 1786 and by 1890 there were 162 reservations, mainly west of the Mississippi.)

Many of the Indian leaders of that time saw the futility of trying to further combat the whites who held the reins of power. They advocated to their people that children must be sent to school, that the new way would be best, and Indians should accept the changes.

Among these were such outstanding men as Quanah Parker of the Comanches, Geronimo of the Apaches, Ouray of the Utes, Chief Joseph of the Nez Perce. All of these men had been warriors of great ability; they now set the example for their people in ways of peace. Some, such as Chief Spokan

Garry of the Spokanes and Sarah Winnemucca of the Paiutes, founded their own schools.

Progress was slow, however. The general attitude seemed to be that Indians could not be educated beyond menial levels, and schooling for them remained on this level. There were no "assists"—no scholarships or loans—for education beyond the vocational institutions of the period and Indians were not encouraged by whites, or by their own people, to try for higher attainment. Without money and without the educational background, it was extremely difficult for an Indian to enter college, or to advance, even if he did so.

By 1936, the few who had gone forth entirely on their own effort, and who made marks of distinction, were the true trail blazers. It was they who carried the banner of Indian ability to accomplish, and who pounded a wedge into the wall of stereotype which could have defeated them.

Among those who were the acknowledged leaders of the time—the "progressives"—were Dr. Charles A. Eastman (Sioux), Rev. Sherman Coolidge (Arapahoe), Dr. Carlos Montezuma (Apache), Arthur C. Parker (Seneca), Thomas Sloan (Omaha), Henry Roe Cloud (Winnebago). Each one of these individuals has a most unusual story, and a record of foremost achievement. They were "eagle people" who flew to the heights, braving the storms and the winds at great sacrifice. They were respected and admired by white society, looked to with hope by some Indians, and thought of as "turncoats" who had become white and forsaken their Indian heritage by others.

Nevertheless, they were trail blazers and certainly influential in reversing the opinion of whites that Indians should not be educated beyond their ability to comprehend —without any definition of what the "ability to comprehend" actually was. It usually meant they were "not to rise above their place." At the time these people lived, those Indians who had gone to college could be counted on the fingers of the hand.

Dr. Charles Eastman grew up on the Plains when the Sioux were still buffalo hunters. Until he was fifteen, he was raised entirely in the Indian way of life and he had never seen a white man. His father, who had taken part in the Minnesota Sioux Uprising, had been put in prison and was assumed dead, but one day he appeared at the Indian village. Pardoned by President Lincoln, he had taken up homesteading and he came for his son, determined that he would grow up in the white world.

The boy was sent to a mission school, knowing no English. He walked the whole way—250 miles—and often met hostile whites, for this was shortly after the Custer battle took place. At the school, however, he was a good student and went on to Beloit College, Knox College, and eventually to Dartmouth on that school's scholarship arrangement for Indian students.

The young Sioux entered fully into the life at Dartmouth. He was popular and made many friends. When he completed his courses he entered Boston University Medical College. At thirty-three, he became physician to the Sioux people on the Pine Ridge Reservation.

He was at Pine Ridge when the Wounded Knee Massacre took place. The Sioux men, women, and children were mowed down by white soldiers because they had taken part in the Ghost Dance, a religious ceremony, and it was feared there was to be an Indian uprising. When Eastman was sent to care for the wounded who survived, it was one of the most terrible and shocking times in his life.

Other things served to complete his disillusionment, and he retired from government service to private practice in Minneapolis. There he began to write the number of books that were to bring him fame—two of them telling the story of his life.

Later, he became a field secretary for the YMCA, traveling among Indians, and he also represented his people in Washington. He spent some seven years in revising the family names and allotment rolls of the Sioux, a monumental task.

Dr. Eastman was internationally, as well as nationally, noted. He lectured abroad on a number of occasions and was a well-known lecturer throughout this country. He loved and sympathized with the life he had known as a boy, but he was oriented toward the new, and equally at home in it.

Rev. Sherman Coolidge, too, came from the old tribal background. When he was seven years old, he was captured by the Army and adopted by an Army officer, growing up with the man's family, and given the family name.

Coolidge was educated in the public schools of New York City, then at Shattuck Military School, and finally at Seabury Divinity School for the Episcopal ministry. He was a man of deep religious conviction, and he served as priest among his own people in Wyoming. Later, he was in charge of the Episcopal missionary work in western Oklahoma.

Dr. Carlos Montezuma, an Apache, was kidnapped by the Pima Indians when he was a small child. All of his people were killed, and he was sold by the Pimas to an itinerant white photographer who adopted him.

The boy traveled around with this man, and went to school in Brooklyn, New York; Galesburg, Illinois; and Chicago. When the man died, Carlos worked his way through the University of Illinois and entered Chicago Medical College.

He practiced for a while in Chicago and then went into the Indian Service as a reservation physician.

Reservation life was not for him, however. He did not think that Indians should cling to their old ways, but should be free to progress, and he blamed the government for holding them back. His constant plea was "Let my people go."

Leaving the reservation, he went to the Carlisle Indian School in Pennsylvania as resident physician. Here he came under the influence of General Richard Henry Pratt, the founder of the school, and was in complete agreement with Pratt's philosophy to "put the Indian in civilization and keep him there." Indians must sink or swim, Montezuma firmly believed, and in this he was completely unchanging.

After Carlisle, Dr. Montezuma practiced again in Chicago where he was a member of the faculty of Rush Medical School and highly regarded by the medical profession. In his last illness, however, he returned to the reservation to die. He is buried there and a Masonic monument stands at his grave.

Arthur C. Parker was reservation-born into a distinguished Christian Indian family, and one that was of great influence in reservation affairs. An ancestor was said to be a founder of the Iroquois Confederacy, and Parker was also descended from Handsome Lake, the Seneca prophet.

In his boyhood, Arthur was formally adopted by the tribe with ancient ritual and given an Indian name. A member of the Bear Clan, he was also taken into membership in the Little Water Society, one of the most sacred of the secret tribal organizations.

He spent most of his childhood on the Seneca reservation where he became imbued with the old traditions, and this was a major interest of his life. He grew up to become an outstanding anthropologist, ethnologist, and museum director, the founder of the Museum of Arts and Sciences in Rochester, New York. He was often in personal conflict over the two worlds to which he belonged, torn between his identity as a Seneca, with Indians in general, and with white society. He was deeply committed to the Indian cause and a tireless worker for the Indian people.

Thomas Sloan was one of the very first Indian lawyers. He was born and brought up on the Omaha reservation by his grandmother, and at one time he was imprisoned for protesting illegal actions on the part of the Indian agent.

Sloan attended Hampton Indian School and he, too, was impressed with the ideas of the founder of Carlisle, since Hampton followed the policies of General Pratt. He later studied law under a practicing attorney and was admitted to the Nebraska bar. In private practice he specialized in Indian cases and was the Omaha tribal delegate to Washington.

Dr. Henry Roe Cloud was born in a wigwam on the Winnebago reservation in Nebraska. He was a protégé of a highly respected missionary from whom he got the name Roe. He went to a federal school for Indians and then was enabled to attend Mt. Hermon where he prepared for college. He was the first Indian to graduate from Yale. After that, he studied for the ministry, becoming an ordained Presbyterian minister.

Dr. Cloud was always active in tribal affairs, and was chairman of the Winnebago delegation to Washington. Appointed a member of a commission to study Indian schools, he grew more and more interested in Indian education and helped to found a college preparatory school for Indian boys in Wichita. This was the only outlet for academic education for Indians at that time, since all government schools were vocational and did not go beyond the lower grades.

Dr. Cloud's school performed such outstanding work that he was asked to head Haskell Indian School, which was the successor to Carlisle, and to raise it to a higher level. His contributions to Indian education were important and many.

By 1960, many scholarships for college education had been established by the government, interested groups, and tribal bodies, and vocational training was greatly broadened. Today, there are many hundreds of Indians in college, and many have advanced degrees or are studying for them. Indians are found in every vocation and profession, or are successfully operating as businessmen. They are limited only by the limitations they place upon themselves. While they have suffered from prejudice, it has not been to the degree that other minorities have suffered. The attitude has been, primarily, to oversentimentalize where Indians are concerned, seeing them as the "noble Hiawatha," an image to which few could measure up. The prejudiced ones saw them as the "bloodthirsty savage," which was far from a true picture.

As Ruth Muskrat Bronson points out, "Indians are people too," and like any people, they don't come in rigid molds. Mrs. Bronson, now retired, is foremost among Indian women. She was for many years guidance and placement officer for the Bureau of Indian Affairs. A Cherokee from Oklahoma, she has a distinguished record of accomplishment and service.

There are many young voices clamoring to be recognized as leaders and "spokesmen" today—some of them are self-styled spokesmen, and others have established organizations and are working to further specific programs. Some have been built up through newspaper attention and actually have few followers. But this is not to deny their sincerity. They look upon themselves as the Pontiacs, the Crazy Horses, and the Geronimos of their people come back to life as protectors and defenders, and they believe that it is only through a dramatic approach that public attention will be captured and focused.

Among the young activists, the following should be mentioned: Clyde Warrior, one of the first, who was the idol of his associates and the spark plug who generated the young people's movement; Lehman Brightman, who has been working for his Ph.D. and who is one of the most extreme in militancy; Tillie Walker, a leader of the Indian contingent in the Washington Protest March of the Poor; Richard Oakes, who stormed the walls of Alcatraz and was the spokesman for the group "in residence" there; Mike Chosa, who has raised considerable havoc in Chicago by taking over various land sites; Russell Means, who founded the American Indian Movement; Grace Thorpe, who is active in attempts to secure surplus lands for Indians.

The current trend among some of these young people has been to do away with tribal identification in favor of Indian identification only, as a symbol of unity and nationalism. Hence, their tribes have not been given. It is interesting to note, however, that Grace Thorpe is the daughter of the famous athlete, Jim Thorpe, who was deprived of his Olympic trophies after winning more events than any other person, because he had once played on a small professional baseball team.

This book presents the biographies of a mere handful of noteworthy Indians of today. Many more personalities could be added—Maria and Marjorie Tallchief, the Osage sisters

who became world-famous ballerinas, Maria one of the greatest of all American dancers; N.B. Johnson, Cherokee, who
was an Oklahoma Supreme Court Chief Justice; Russell
Moore, Pima, and Buffy Ste. Marie, Cree, both noted as jazz
musician and folk singer; Dr. Gilbert Monture, Mohawk,
and world authority on mineral economy; Colonel Ernest
Childers, Creek, and Congressional Medal of Honor winner;
Wilma Victor, Choctaw, who is special assistant to the Secretary of the Interior. The list is a long one.

The biographies included here present a wide variety of
viewpoints and a cross section of vocations. The individuals
range from the extremely militant to the conservative and the
in-between. There are the traditionalists and the progressives,
the young and the elder, those of the reservation and those
of urban background. Each deserves to be called a contemporary Indian leader.

Henry (Hank) Adams

Henry adams is one of the more militant of the young Indian militants. He has been dedicated to fighting for Indian rights since he was twenty and, as such, he has become a highly controversial figure.

Hank was born on the Assiniboine Reservation at Fort Peck, Montana, in 1944. His home town of Wolf Point is more often referred to as Poverty Flats. It is in the heart of the Plains, surrounded by grazing lands. A few of the Indian people have good ranches, but the Adams family was not one of these.

Hank's father was a topflight rodeo cowboy who entered military service and was sent overseas when Hank was eighteen months old. His mother moved to the west coast, with others from the reservation, to work in a defense plant. When his father returned from the Army, the family lived in Oregon where the father found work with the railroads and the mother worked in a hospital. Then there was a divorce and his mother remarried, and then another divorce and remarriage, this time to a Quinault Indian from Taholah, Washington.

Coupled with the emotional trauma of the two breakups,

the separation from his own father, and the removal to a new country, there was the death of an older sister in a hunting accident. Still, Hank managed to become one of the best students in the history of the high school he attended. He graduated with a perfect 4.0 grade-point average, and in the course of his schooling was student body president, editor of the school newspaper and annual, and a star athlete, excelling in football and basketball.

He attended the University of Washington, but did not graduate. He dropped out before the end of his second year because he was generally dissatisfied with college. He quit school on the day that President Kennedy was shot.

Shortly before entering college, Hank had been bitten by politics. He had gone to California to work for Richard M. Nixon in his campaign for governor, then was attracted to John F. Kennedy, who became his idol. The death of Kennedy was deeply disturbing.

Another disturbing factor was that some of his young friends had committed suicide. And he was concerned about other problems too. The Quinaults were in conflict with the surrounding whites. There was little respect for the Indians or for their property. Visitors using the fine reservation beaches left them in a shambles. They raced their speedboats over Indian waters, disturbing the salmon and other fish, and this was detrimental to Indian fishing. Protests were largely ignored until the Tribal Council took drastic action and closed reservation lands to whites.

Burning with resentment, Hank was determined to be active in Indian causes. He could not remain just an onlooker.

Then came the matter of Indian fishing rights, with open war declared between the Indians of several tribes and the state of Washington. The issue was over Indian treaty rights and state conservation efforts.

The Indians of the Puget Sound area had fished the various waters from time immemorial. These rights were reserved to them by the United States government in a treaty made long before there was a state of Washington.

The state claimed that since at that time there was not a state, the state was not bound by the treaty. The Indians claimed that the treaty was for all time, and that the fact that it was made with the federal government took precedence over any state rulings.

The state chose to disregard this, and barred Indians from fishing unless they complied with state regulations. It was said that Indian fishing methods were harmful and endangering the salmon. The Indians claimed that the state was acting only in the interests of white sports and commercial fishermen. Fishing was an economic necessity for the Indians, yet tribes were wholly and totally prevented from fishing on their accustomed grounds and in their accustomed ways.

Whites, it was stated, had averaged an annual salmon catch of more than 6,000,000 salmon each year since 1935. It was pointed out that one expedition by one white commercial fishing boat caught more salmon than any one of the tribes involved out of any given run.

To all of this, the state turned a deaf ear, and matters quickly progressed to a screaming, shooting, open revolution. The screams from the Indian people were of pure hatred, anger, and a lust for revenge. The federal government brought suit in the Indians' behalf, and some individual tribes took the same action in their own, but this offered no immediate relief. Going to law is a long, slow process.

The fishing rights struggle attracted such public figures

as Marlon Brando and Dick Gregory. Brando personally led 1,000 Indians and their supporters in a protest march to the state capitol. While these things were taking place, Hank Adams was a behind-the-scenes observer. He met with the protesting Indians, however, formed friendships among them, and strongly favored them.

"The state has only one aim," he said. "I don't care what kind of public statements it makes. It intends to destroy our fishing equipment, chase us off the rivers, and save the fish for the white men."

Hank was now to emerge as a "protestant" in another way. He refused to be drafted as long as the Indian treaty rights were ignored. He did serve in the Army, however.

"Indians don't need the draft," he commented at one time. "As one whose great-grandfathers fought in the historic battle to defeat the U.S. Seventh Cavalry [Hank is part Sioux and it is the Sioux who were engaged in the battle with Custer], and whose father suffered wounds in World War II, and as one who has resisted the draft yet served in the Army, I find a constancy of values in the military experience of my own family and hold a firm belief that we are always on the right side."

Hank, by then, was a plaintiff in a suit which asked that Indian men be exempt from federal draft laws. The suit, he said, "would restore a condition which existed at the time of World War I when Indians were not subject to the draft nor obligated to serve in the military, yet they volunteered for such service in proportionately greater numbers than any other racial segment of the population."

It was his feeling that Indians, as the "first Americans," should retain a status of nondraftable people and that they would continue to volunteer for military service out of love of country. Indians should be free to serve but not made to do so, was his thinking.

In 1968, Hank was director of an antipoverty community action program on the Quillieute Reservation in Washington. He became very much engrossed in the problems of the poor and this led him to journey to Washington as one of the organizers of the Indian participation in the Poor People's March. He was in the forefront of an episode in which the Indians stoned the United States Supreme Court building in protest over the fishing rights and other issues. For this, he spent a number of weeks in jail.

Working for the National Indian Youth Council and the National Congress of American Indians in employment and scholarship programs, Hank found this lacking in the "gutsy approach." He wanted to be where the action was. So, when asked to become director of the Survival of American Indians Association, a group of about 200 young militants pledged to work in the American treaty-fishing rights battle, he said a quick "yes." This group, in fact, had been the instigators of the first fishing rights protest activity.

Hank was now fully dedicated to the battle. He became so active that he aroused considerable hatred among his opponents. He was scorned and reviled, arrested and put in jail a number of times. All of this he expected and was willing to endure, saying to his followers: "If we are renegades, it is because we are right—so, as long as we are right, let's be renegades."

In trying to explain why he was so immersed in the cause, he said: "The fishing right is one of the most vital and valid treaty rights still existing. It is valid for changing the life of Indians. Treaties are abstract for the most part, almost meaningless except for a few essential elements. One of these is our sovereignty. The self-government part of treaties is the most basic of all . . . the fishing right gives the Indian people that type of tribal community which is necessary. The problem existing has to be resolved."

About one of his arrests, Hank states that he was only helping a group of Nisqually Indians to unsnag a net. He was seized and lodged in jail on a charge of illegal fishing. This charge was later reversed.

He was again charged with illegal fishing when he was giving the only political speech he ever made. This charge, too, was reversed, but Hank now went nowhere without a gun.

"I have seen too many Indians who have not had the right to live on even a small parcel of land protected by treaty," he said. "We have to protect our rights, and ourselves, with guns, but we don't like to rely on that protection for our treaty. There is vigilantism on our rivers and a steady stream of vigilantes at our trials, pointing us out as troublemakers. We have been attacked and beaten and our women and children endangered."

At this time, Hank had begun another concerted campaign to defy state regulation of Indian fishing methods and state conservation officers. While he was sitting in a car on a bank above the Puyallup River, watching a net for steelhead trout fishing, a shot rang out. Hank doubled over from a bullet which entered his body close to the navel, curved around vital organs, and went out at his side. Hospitalized, he found himself accused of inflicting his own wound in order to throw suspicion on others. He refused to take a lie test and the matter was never settled.

With regard to this affair, Hank commented: "I think I was shot by an attitude more than anything else. I think the state has really created a hatred and hostility among elements of the public by not informing them of all the issues in the Indian fishing situation. I think I was shot simply because no one, other than a few Indians, has tried to resolve the fishing rights dispute." He also pointed out that it would be very difficult for anyone to shoot himself in that manner unless intent on taking his own life.

Recovered from his wound, Hank held a press conference, charging that Indians were being harassed and would protect themselves. If anything, the shooting intensified his own feelings and commitment. He organized efforts to get a better market price for Indian-caught fish, sending shipments direct to the New York wholesalers. He also announced that he intended to bring together resources from a lot of prominent people in the country who would assist in a program that would end the "era of fear" for the Indians in Washington State.

The fact that he accepted assistance from outside groups, from "Yippies" to black militants, and others, brought down upon him much criticism from many of his own people. He was labeled "deeper than pink" by more conservative Indians who disclaimed him as a leader. This he shrugged off, saying, "I will continue to protest and to hold protests until matters are righted, no matter what the 'Uncle Tomahawks' and the 'red apples' say."

The term "Uncle Tomahawk" is a paraphrase of the Negroes' "Uncle Tom," and the "red apple" is one who is of red skin, but white on the inside.

Early in 1972, Hank announced that he would take a group of Indian people to North Vietnam in response to an invitation from the Hanoi government's Committee for Solidarity with the American People. Undoubtedly this has added fuel to the fire of adverse opinion, but Hank justifies the trip, financed by East Coast church groups active in the peace movement, in this fashion: "We go to Vietnam as pro-American Indian people, holding, however, a judgment that America has been predominantly wrong in its role in Vietnam. We're not anti-American. Indians in the United States have a more favored position than Indian people in virtually any other country in the Western Hemisphere— Canada, Mexico, and Central America, and South America."

He cited two endangering factors to the trip—the hostility of the Communist Party in the United States to some of the stated positions of the Indian delegation and the possible intrusion of alien viewpoints and rhetoric by intermediary peace groups upon the Indian delegation.

He also said that the group would request visits throughout the Indo-Chinese peninsula "to speak with people of position and policy-making authority in Laos, South Vietnam, and Cambodia as well.

"I would hope our trip will generate some thought among Indian people," he says. "I would think that those Indians who are looking to their leaders, fighters, and heroes among generalized and tribal histories should have the capacity to understand what a Ho Chi Minh means to his people in both North and South Vietnam."

Louis W. Ballard

U<small>NTIL</small> Louis Ballard appeared on the scene, no American Indian had penetrated the field of music as a composer of recognized talent. Louis Ballard has become one of the "greats" in his field, a constant winner of awards and honors, and a constant producer of music. He is the only person, Indian or non-Indian, to bring American Indian music into the twentieth century.

Music has always been secondary to art in studies of Indian culture, and to establish a new American musical tradition which remains close to the tribal spirit is a highly difficult task. Louis Ballard has brought Indian music into the mainstream as our purest body of American folk music and has done this alone by projecting his work through classrooms and the concert stage.

Ballard's mother was Quapaw-French, his father Cherokee-Scotch with an ancestry going back to William the Conqueror and the invasion of the British Isles. William asked for singers of battle songs to come forth, and a Gaulish family of ballad singers answered the call. Later, they settled and lived in Scotland where they became known as the Ballards, from the word "ballad."

The Ballards in America all trace themselves back to this family, which has a family crest and the motto "to hold the banner high." The first American Ballards settled in Virginia and Kentucky. They married among the Cherokees, and the Indian Ballards were noted for scholastic attainment. Many of them became educators.

Louis Ballard was born at Miami, Oklahoma. When very young, he was placed in the care of his grandmother, who directed his interests to music and education.

Near his grandmother's home, there was a little mission church and she loved to hear the church pianist and the choir singers each Sunday. She decided that her grandson should also "make music," and so, at six, young Louis began his music lessons.

His mother had been a talented pianist and composed little songs for her children and pieces for the piano. Louis, remembering this, enjoyed his music lessons and took to them with relish.

In Oklahoma there are a large number of Indian tribes and each possesses its rich oral traditions of music and mythology. Tribal dances and ceremonials were held regularly and Louis was often in attendance at these affairs. He absorbed this native music and learned the songs and dances as did any other young Indian boy.

As his musical education continued, he became an accomplished pianist and composer, with his creative efforts reflecting both Indian and white cultures. Indian melodies pulsed throughout his music, giving it a character and tempo that were distinctive.

When Louis enrolled at the University of Tulsa, he found, under the influence of his teacher, that he was utilizing every contemporary technique from the impressionism of Debussy to the serialism of Schoenberg in order to find a style that would best express his own musical ideas.

He continued his musical studies under great teachers—Castelnuovo-Tedesco, Darius Milhaud, Carlos Surinach, and others—and was much impressed by Béla Bartók, who composed music based upon the spirit of an ethnic race of people, the Hungarians.

"Why can't I do the same for my people?" Louis mused. But first, he had to steep himself in every aspect of the culture, the dances, the songs, the language, the customs—and from this he had to develop his own identification as a musician based upon the embodiment of the Indian spirit.

There had been composers such as Charles Cadman and Thurlow Lieurance who had attempted to blend Indian melodies with Caucasian style, but the essence of what made Indian music was missing. It was like making apple pie without the apples, or pumpkin pie without the spice.

Louis determined that his music would be truer to the emotional climate of the Indian than the works of any other composer. Indian music as it exists in the primitive form cannot be accurately notated, and any attempt to rewrite it is futile, he says. Therefore, his music became his own personal response and approach to the cultural blend of Indian and non-Indian.

Ballard's education was not obtained easily. He worked as a dishwasher, an ambulance driver, drug store clerk, waiter, undertaker, bar room piano player, vocal accompanist, and janitor. These were the means to an end—his desire to win for his people's music an appreciation and recognition that had been denied. Nothing was to stand in the way of that ambition.

And so, when the dances were held in Oklahoma, a tall,

young figure strode out to the center to dance with dignity and to find in this participation his Indian roots. He listened carefully to the singers and his ear quickly caught and held the cadences and tones, the rhythmic breaks and changes, and the melodic patterns that were unique.

He began to collect many different types of Indian songs and today has a collection numbering in the hundreds. He has beautiful chants from the Southwest, the stirring music of the Plains, the staccato woodland melodies, and the rolling tones from the Northwest coast. He has lullabies, love songs, dream songs, ceremonial songs, and dance songs by the score.

From these songs, Louis obtained the inspiration for his piano preludes, chamber music, orchestral works, and ballet music. He has written a collection of percussion pieces, string and woodwind trios, cello and piano duets, music for decorative drums, choral cantatas, orchestral and instrumental concert pieces. He has also written much classroom material—all of it Indian in theme.

Ballard earned his music Master's degree in 1967. A year later he received his first commission from the Santa Fe symphony orchestra. Other commissions followed in quick order.

Even then, his agile mind was already engaged in producing the music for a ballet based on the creation of the world as seen through the eyes of the Hopi Indians. *Koshare* is the first ballet composed by an Indian, and it was premièred by the Harkness Ballet Company in Spain at the famed Teatro Liceo of Barcelona. The American opening was in Washington before a select group of government and civic dignitaries.

The Four Moons, another ballet, was a mystical presentation danced for the state of Oklahoma's sixtieth anniversary

in 1967. It featured four noted Indian ballerinas—Marjorie
Tallchief, Moscelyne Larkin, Yvonne Choteau, and Rosella
Hightower, all internationally famous and all natives of
Oklahoma.

Still another ballet, *Why the Duck Has a Short Tail,* based
on a Navajo folk story, has had over a hundred performances
to date and has been favorably compared to *Peter and the
Wolf.* It is rapidly attaining the status of a children's classic,
and has been played by a number of prominent symphony
orchestras, among them the Children's Concert Series of the
Philadelphia Symphony Orchestra. The work includes nar-
ration, chant, and Indian instruments within the framework
of the original, contemporary score, something never before
attempted. A ballet version was performed by a San Francisco company on tour in the Far East and at Expo '70 in
Japan. This music is to be recorded in an album of other
compositions of Louis Ballard and a Foundation is to be
established to administer scholarships for music students.

Yet to come is a chamber work with chorus and/or vocalist
on the life of Kateri Tekakwitha, the Mohawk girl who was
one of the first Christian converts and who has been proposed
for sainthood. It is to be entered in competition in Europe.
Also, an opera, based on an Indian story, is to be premièred
in the John F. Kennedy Center in Washington.

In 1969, Ballard was the first to receive the Marion Nevins
MacDowell Award for his woodwind quintet, *Ritmo Indio.*
This was commissioned and first performed by the Dorian
Woodwind Quintet through a Rockefeller Foundation grant.
Of all the many honors that have come his way, this, per-
haps, is the most meaningful since it is one of the highest
musical honors. In 1966, he received an ASCAP composer's
award and has received one annually through 1970.

In 1971 there were other signal honors. The University of Colorado sponsored a conference on Indian music which featured Ballard and his works, and the United States Army Band and Soldiers' Chorus included his *Scenes from Indian Life* in its world premiere in Santa Fe. Ballard was the first Indian so honored.

Again, Texas Technical University's twenty-first annual Symposium of Contemporary Music, held as part of the International Center's Festival of the Arts of the Americas, featured Ballard, whose *Desert Trilogy* was commissioned especially for the Festival. Other of his works were also included.

At the year's end, Louis was invited to present an ethnic music evening at the White House by the Music Educators National Conference, in conjunction with the White House Conference on Children and Youth.

For this, he wrote a composition overnight entitled *Mid-Winter Fires*, which celebrates the ceremonials of the Eastern Woodland Indians. The work was a bicultural composition, utilizing a clarinet, Indian flute, and piano.

The performers taped the composition in one day and it was sent to the MENC for approval. The confirmation of the White House appearance arrived immediately thereafter.

Louis Ballard goes by the dignified title of Musicethnocologist, yet this hardly conveys the depth of his activities or the outreach of his tremendous talent. He is dean of the music department of the Institute of Indian Arts in Santa Fe and music curriculum specialist for the Bureau of Indian Affairs, responsible for the entire music teaching program in government Indian schools.

So much of Indian culture has been lost that Louis Ballard has found that many of his pupils have no knowledge of the songs of their people and no idea of how to sing them. A perfectionist, he is a hard taskmaster. He insists that the pure sense and values of Indian music be brought forth. He tells his students that each chant must be sung as well, or better, than the tribal musician to whom it belongs. Every syllable, vocal stress, and subtle nuance must be mastered; the separate style of each tribe must be identified and retained. How people sing is as meaningful as what they sing, he says.

"My life has been doubly enriched because I have lived in two worlds—two cultures," Louis Ballard says. "Because I identify with my Indian background, my creative expression has been enhanced and extended to others."

With a record like this, there is no doubt that Louis Ballard is a gifted leader, and one with even greater accomplishment to come. He has not only set a high musical mark, but he has brought about an appreciation and understanding of Indian music that has not previously existed.

It takes a lot of work and much creative ability to communicate to others in a virtually unknown element. Music teachers, and people in general, have shied away from authentic Indian melodies, probably because of the unfamiliar sounds which are too often considered harsh and disagreeable. They have been concerned with the content of Indian songs rather than their style.

But without sacrifice of the original melodies, Louis Ballard has brought Indian music forward and helped people to enjoy it. And ovations by audiences do not come without justification.

Robert L. Bennett

On March 18, 1966, an announcement of great importance to the Indian people was made by President Lyndon B. Johnson. This was the appointment of Robert La-Follett Bennett, an Oneida Indian, born on the reservation in 1912, as Commissioner of Indian Affairs.

The announcement was of major interest because the Bureau of Indian Affairs, which the Commissioner heads, controls the lives and destinies of some 800,000 Indians and natives of Alaska from the "cradle to the grave." It is the largest government agency in the Department of the Interior and is responsible for the administration of Indian properties, trust funds, educational and employment programs, economic assistance, self-development and assistance projects.

Some Indian reservations are very large and some very small. Some tribes have great wealth and others are extremely poor; some are more advanced than others. Whatever their condition and status, Indians, with few exceptions, come under this governmental bureau.

At the time of Bennett's appointment, the Indian Bureau was under severe attack. Indians strongly protested the policy of telling them what to do, or what would be done, in the manner of a strict father speaking to his children. They wanted the opportunity to express their own feelings and desires and to be directly involved in any programs affecting them.

As he stood in the White House to be sworn in by Secretary Stewart Udall in the presence of President and Mrs. Johnson, the pleasant-faced, well-built man with slightly graying hair heard the President predict that he would be the "greatest of all Indian Commissioners." The President said that he was to have complete authority over making a clean sweep in the Indian Bureau and to do whatever he thought needed to be done. It was an impressive statement.

President Johnson's remarks were awesome, for they expressed complete confidence in the abilities of the Oneida who stood before him, and whom he had called from an assignment in Alaska to assume the Commissionership. As he heard them, Robert Bennett reflected over the past experiences that had brought him this high honor. It seemed that he had been in training for it from the day he entered Haskell Indian School.

He was not the first Indian to be Commissioner of Indian Affairs. One hundred years before, General Ely S. Parker, a Seneca who was aide to General Ulysses Grant, had held the office. But Robert was extremely qualified for the tremendous responsibility he was to carry. He was the first Indian Commissioner born and raised on a federal Indian reservation; he had lived among his people all of his life; he had attended a government Indian school; and throughout his career he had worked with many tribes. He was also the first BIA employee to rise through the ranks to the top position.

And he had grown up in the middle of two worlds—Indian

and white—and he knew that this could be an emotionally disturbing way of life. "Young Indian people must learn to live in two worlds so as not to become the victims of both," he was to say later in life. He successfully accomplished this.

The Oneida Indians were one of the original tribes of the great Iroquois Confederacy, so skilled in statesmanship and in organization. The Confederacy was never equalled by any other Indian group. It held sway in northeast America for three hundred years, and parts of the Constitution of this country bear the imprint of the Iroquois governmental structure.

The Oneidas moved from their New York lands to Wisconsin in the 1800's where they purchased new lands for themselves. Their reservation is so small that Bennett often says with a twinkle, "When you come to Oneida, there is a sign that reads, 'You are now on the Oneida reservation.' On looking backward, you will read the reverse lettering: 'You have now passed through the Oneida Reservation.'"

Robert's grandmother still lived during his boyhood. She spoke no English, was entirely Indian in her thinking, and highly resistant to white ways and white schooling. She had refused to send her eight children to school but was finally haled into court and ordered to do so. This she protested strenuously and was finally able to secure a compromise from the judge. She was allowed to keep her four oldest children out of school but she was required to send her four youngest. One of these children was Robert's mother, who went through high school.

In his boyhood years, Robert lived with his parents in a small house at the edge of a woods. His father wrestled with the swampland in an attempt at farming which eventually failed. The family then moved into the Oneida community and the father worked at odd jobs. His mother was a leader among her people and often acted as interpreter for those who could not speak English.

She firmly believed that Robert must learn to live according to white custom, and she saw to it that he learned to speak English and not the Oneida tongue. She was proud of the knowledge and skill as a seamstress which she had attained at school and she counseled her son that he too must have a respect for education. She had not been separated from her people, she pointed out, but was able to help them where they could not help themselves. She said that both Indian and white ways of life held much good, and that her son must draw upon the best in each.

When he was old enough, Robert's mother entered him in a private school where he was an Indian among many whites. But he was popular with his classmates and his friendly manner won him many friends. He was active in a number of school events and he was elected to various class offices. When he returned to the Oneidas, he was just as popular among the Indian boys, for he was always proud of being an Indian.

Robert's father died when he was fifteen, and attendance at the private school had to end. There was little money, and so his mother arranged for him to go to Haskell, the government boarding school in Kansas. It was the best she could do for her son, for there were other children to support. So he went away with only one pair of levis, a shirt, and his shoes. There was no help to be had through tribal resources, and there was no educational assistance for Indians at that time to carry him on through college. Whatever he accomplished had to be done entirely through his own efforts.

He spent five and a half years at Haskell where he came

in contact with Indian students from all over the country. He began to understand that Indians had problems in common, no matter where they were from—problems specific to their own tribes and areas. He began to feel that it was the obligation of younger Indians to do something about resolving them. Younger Indians owed it to their people, he felt, to gain knowledge and education, not only so that they could enter another way of life, but so that they would be equipped to deal with Indian-government relationships. Above all, he felt that they must hold onto their dignity and racial pride.

When Bennett graduated, the depression of the '30's was intensifying. Jobs were scarce for everyone and even scarcer for Indians. When he was offered a clerkship at Haskell, he accepted with alacrity, even though it paid only $1.00 a day plus his room and board. Shortly thereafter, he was promoted to junior clerk and transferred to the Bureau headquarters in Washington. He welcomed this as an opportunity to learn about government service from the inside, and as a stepping-stone to helping his people.

The first assignment of consequence was with the Ute Agency where he worked in various capacities with the Ute Tribal Council. He was also treasurer of three Indian live-stock associations.

When he returned to Washington as tribal specialist, he enrolled in law school, attending classes for three years from 6:30 A.M. to 8:30 P.M., before going to work. He was married, with a wife and three children to support on a meager salary. Getting ahead was a burning desire and acquiring the white man's knowledge was a commitment.

After obtaining his degree, Robert was sent to the Navajo Reservation, the largest in the country, as administrative assistant. He remained there until World War II when he entered the Marine Corps. Returning from this duty, he directed a training program for World War II Indian veterans as a member of the Veterans Administration. Through his efforts, several hundred Indian GI's were enabled to get their education under the GI program. He also organized the Navajo and Ute American Legion Posts.

Once again with the Bureau of Indian Affairs as a placement officer, he arranged the first agreements with a state employment agency for special services for South Dakota Indians.

Reassigned to Washington, he assisted in the development of tribal programs, and then became superintendent of the Consolidated Ute Agency. His next position was that of Assistant Area Director, stationed at Aberdeen, South Dakota, and from there he went to Juneau, Alaska, as Area Director. There he initiated three studies aimed to develop native resources. While there, too, he was chosen to receive the Indian Achievement Award, an honor first established at the Chicago Century of Progress in 1933 and given for achievement in the face of difficulties or for humanitarian endeavor. Bennett qualified on both counts.

And so he came to the moment when he heard the pronouncement of President Johnson and pledged himself anew as an Indian to work for the betterment of his race. He stressed again that Indians must face life in their time, drawing on the past but not resting on it.

"Let us continue to honor that which remains only in dream memory," he said. "But do not permit it to blind us to the present reality. To build upon the past is a challenge to wits and to wisdom. It is one which Indians should be able to meet successfully."

In a sense, by his appointment, it was acknowledged that Indians had "grown up," and Bennett set out at once to clear the weeds of established bureaucracy and patronization that had so long dominated the scene. He intended to focus on improving the education of Indian children and encouraging attendance in public schools.

Before his confirmation as Commissioner, Bennett was subjected to intensive questioning by the Senate Interior and Insular Committee. The nature of the questioning was so probing that a Senator was heard to comment, "Now you know, Mr. Bennett, how Custer must have felt."

Bennett passed this grueling interview with flying colors, but he was ordered to submit a written report within three months of his confirmation on what has been done to insure that "Indians are released from unnecessary bureaucracy, entanglement, and outdated controls."

This statement made many Indians uneasy, seeing it as a threat to terminate government services and administration, although agreeing that this was a goal toward which Indians should be encouraged to work.

While there was genuine rejoicing among Indian people across the country at Bennett's selection—for he had earned a reputation for forthrightness and speaking up for Indians in the face of unpopular policies—there were some Indians who saw in him the "government man." As he visited tribe after tribe to meet with them and get their views, Bennett was often questioned unmercilessly.

The Navajos, for one, bluntly asked if he would carry out the wishes of the Interior Department, or of the Indians. The answer was quick and sincere. "If the Secretary of the Interior and I had serious disagreement on matters of policy, I would have to resign. I will not give up my personal philosophy for a job."

Later, the Navajos went on record with this comment: "If his personal philosophy is honest, as we believe it to be, he will be a fine Commissioner; or, if he tangles with his superiors, he may be the shortest one on record in time of service. Either way, he would have our respect."

In a speech the day before his swearing-in, Robert Bennett laid it on the line. "A way through the morass of Indian problems must be found and federal administrators cannot do it alone. Satisfactory solutions may be found only with the fullest cooperation of all levels of government in concert with Indian people themselves. The ultimate answers must be the result of voluntary decisions by the Indian people . . . what we need now is to draw Indian people to the conference tables . . . the paternalistic approach is good no longer. It has resulted in a culture of poverty, and even at best encourages a dependency approach to life."

Once in office, there was a tremendous outpouring of honors and gifts from Indians for the new Commissioner. Robert was taken into secret and ritualistic societies, had honorary names conferred upon him, was adopted into tribes, and received gifts ranging from beadwork, pottery, and baskets to the eagle feather war bonnet, the highest honor of all.

While in office, Bennett developed the first Presidential message on Indian affairs ever sent to the Congress of the United States. He succeeded in gaining the support of all governmental agencies that had programs affecting Indians and, with their cooperation, set up the National Commission on Indian Opportunity in the office of the Vice President of the United States. Its purpose is to watch over programs initiated for Indians to make certain that they are of actual help and not window dressing, or with ulterior motive.

Bennett also launched a program which would eventually give the tribes the responsibility for all the services then being provided by the Bureau. The plan was that Indians would run their own schools, direct their own medical programs and housing programs, and take on many other activities which were then the sole province of the Bureau.

While he was still in office, there was a movement to terminate Indian tribes from federal services, but he knew that this could come only very gradually. Many tribes were still not ready to be completely on their own. He fought the powerful interests and the men who were determined to embark on this course, and he was able to prevent it altogether for a number of tribes that were seriously threatened.

As Commissioner of Indian Affairs, Robert Bennett proved to the government and to the American people that Indians had come of age in the white man's world and were capable citizens. He also demonstrated to Indians that it was possible to live in two worlds by accepting the best of both. He changed the settled ways of the Bureau that had been entrenched for more than a hundred years. He encouraged the Indian spirit to remain strong and the people to preserve their arts and crafts, their music and traditions, so that they would not be lost forever.

He was the first Commissioner to travel over the United States and Alaska, to visit and communicate with many tribes, and to meet with many Indian leaders. He listened, rather than talked, and he understood in ways that no one else could.

With the change in administration, Mr. Bennett's career with the Indian Bureau came to an end, though his service for his people did not. He became Director of the Indian School of Law at the University of New Mexico. He guides Indian students in their law studies, recruits Indian students, and works to improve the legal status of Indians.

He has initiated research projects that will take legal means to help Indians in their long struggle to cope with the intricate and involved "legalities" which have hampered them for many years. And always he counsels: "If we take up our option to be critical, then we must also assume the responsibility to be constructively critical . . . Before we become known as just another minority group with a gripe but no grip on ourselves, let us appraise ourselves objectively. People must talk and listen to each other with mutual respect and a desire for understanding. To be part of the total community does not require one to be less Indian. We must not look backward in anger, but forward with definite goals in mind."

George Blue Spruce

GEORGE BLUE SPRUCE is the nation's only full-blood Indian dentist and the only Indian dentist in the Public Health Service. He comes from Santa Fe, New Mexico, where he was born in 1931. His parents were from the San Juan and Laguna pueblos.

Neither of George's grandparents could read or write, but his father and mother had gone to school. His father taught drafting and cabinetmaking at the government Indian school in Santa Fe, and his mother was a cook at the institution. Both were ambitious for their son and they wanted more for him than the government school offered at that time.

The boy was enrolled in a parochial school, and from the first he was an apt scholar. From the third grade through high school, he was on every honor roll. The fact that he was an Indian in a non-Indian school at times meant for moments of anguish. But he refused to be discouraged and in high school his years were filled with honors. He was class president in both his junior and senior years, and he was valedictorian of his graduating class.

George recalls a conversation with his father and mother when he was still in ninth grade. He was remembering a painful dental experience with a non-Indian dentist in an Indian health clinic. The man seemed to have little sympathy for his patients, and little understanding of the fright that Indians, unfamiliar with dental care, could experience.

His parents encouraged him to believe that he should enter this profession. Dental care was badly needed by Indians and an Indian dentist could be influential in helping them to get it.

A student counselor, however, advised him that dentistry was a poor choice. It was difficult to get into a dental school, he said, and only rich, white boys could do so.

When George graduated from high school he was awarded a $300 scholarship by the New Mexico Elks Association as the winner of a competitive state-wide contest for outstanding high school students.

He was asked to come to the association's annual state convention to receive the award, and he told of his desire to become a dentist and his feelings that it would not be possible for him to pursue this career.

"My family is poor," he said, "and there is no way for them to help me."

Touched by the boy, so obviously of superior intelligence, and so handicapped by circumstances, the Grand Exalted Ruler of the Elks made a special plea. Before the evening was over the various lodges had pledged financial support sufficient to secure George's entire seven-year college and dental education.

Looking back, George Blue Spruce is overwhelmed by the miracle which took place, for it was truly that—or rather, people helping to bring about a miracle. He entered Creighton University where he received his dental degree in 1956.

Before he received his D.D.S., he served in the Navy as a dentist.

To get experience, George opened private practice in Santa Fe. He then entered the U.S. Public Health Service and was dental officer with the Indian Health Service at Taos, New Mexico, one of the most traditional of the conservative Indian pueblos. He was then transferred to the reservation at Fort Belknap, Montana.

The young Indian dentist made an impression on his own people, who became more responsive to "going to the dentist." Resistances began to break down in those areas where he was stationed. He made an impression on his superiors, too, and he was sent to the Public Health Service outpatient clinic in New York City as a dental resident, to round out and broaden his training. In a short time, he became Deputy Chief of this clinic.

For a three-year period, George was Chief Dental Officer at the U.S. Merchant Marine Academy in New York and then was sent to the Dental Health Center in San Francisco. Here he developed and tested a mobile dental clinic for Indian children in Nevada. While in California, he studied for his Master's degree in public health, one of very few dentists in the Indian health program to hold this degree.

Throughout his career, George wrote a number of papers about his experiences with Indians. One paper, "American Indians as Dental Patients," received the first-prize Surgeon General's Award for the best paper presented at the annual meeting of Public Health Physicians and Dentists.

Dr. Blue Spruce speaks before many national, state, and local groups on dental health programs for Indians, with special emphasis on Indian customs, cultures, attitudes, and beliefs.

"These must all be taken into consideration by anyone working in Indian health programs," he points out. "It is only by doing so that confidence and cooperation can be won. It is a constant challenge to those who go into this branch of service."

Dr. Blue Spruce, when named as a Consultant in Dental Health for the Pan-American Health Organization, gave instruction in the use of dental auxiliaries and the fabrication of simplified equipment for dentistry in primitive areas. He visited most of the countries of South America where he found the native dental situation to be as appalling, if not more so than it was in the States. His aim was to help dentists who would be working in remote and jungle areas with no modern equipment find ways to treat the people with things that could be fashioned from the materials at hand.

Returning to Washington, he became Chief of the Auxiliary Utilization Section of the Education Development Branch, Division of Dental Health, Bureau of Health Manpower Education, National Institutes of Health. This office was responsible for providing grants and technical aids to dental schools for two programs—dental auxiliary utilization and training in expanded auxiliary management.

Because of his marked zeal for the recruitment of minority students into health professions, Dr. Blue Spruce was appointed, in 1971, to head a major new program to improve the health of the American Indians. He was named a Special Assistant to the director of HEW's Bureau of Health Manpower Education to recruit Indians into the various health professions in cooperation with the Indian Health Service. "This is a giant step forward to expand the effort to train Indians for health programs," Dr. Blue Spruce says.

The job would not be easy, he knew, but he said: "This

is an endeavor that is going to have to be assumed by every-one, starting with the Indian student's parents and including the tribal community and his primary and secondary school teachers."

Remembering how his parents had encouraged him, even though they came from pueblos which at that time were backward in their attitudes about progress, Dr. Blue Spruce lays particular stress on Indian willingness to enter the health professions. Because he did so, a brother, Dr. Beryl Blue Spruce, was inspired to become a physician and is an in-structor at the University of Michigan School of Public Health.

"Of the nation's 118,000 dentists, I am the only one who has been identified as a full-blood Indian," he says. "Of the 317,000 physicians and osteopaths, only thirty-eight have been identified as Indian. And no Indians have been identi-fied among the nation's 25,000 veterinarians and 8,000 podi-atrists. There are no Indian optometrists."

With increasing national attention being given to minor-ities, the time is ripe for this major effort to help Indians enter medical fields, Dr. Blue Spruce believes. "We want to improve the quality of their lives by getting more of them into all fields related to health, returning them to their own people in terms of a much needed service. We should be able to open new doors for Indians to become health profes-sionals with the department's links with medical institutions, the Indian Health Service's capability to deliver compre-hensive care, and with my own ties to the Indian commu-nity," he states.

A number of programs are already under way. The Indian Health Service has courses for training Indian practical nurses, health record technicians, radiology technicians, dental assistants, sanitarian aides, laboratory assistants, medical social work associates, food service supervisors, nutrition technicians, health educators, mental health workers, community health representatives and community health medics.

On-the-job training is provided for nursing assistants, food service workers, and medical record clerks. Leadership training is offered to prepare Indians to operate their own health programs.

The Bureau of Health Manpower Education, for which Blue Spruce was the two-program director (heading both on-the-job training and leadership training), financed the placement of counselors at Northern Arizona University and Navajo Community College to help place interested Indians in training for health professions with a center for financial aid to such students established in Denver. Summer employment was also arranged for, and a pilot program was started with the University of South Dakota and the Rosebud-Pine Ridge Community College for nursing assistants and licensed practical nurses to work toward an associate nursing degree without leaving their communities.

An accelerated associate nursing degree program was also started by the Phoenix Indian Medical Center, Arizona State University School of Nursing, and Maricopa County College System, in which licensed practical nurses are given credit for previous training and experience.

All of these resources will be available to Dr. Blue Spruce as he forges his program of Indian recruitment. A first step has been undertaken with the formation of the Association of American Indian Physicians, which will also be put to work in the recruitment of Indians.

Jarrett Blythe

JARRETT BLYTHE has held the office of Principal Chief of the Eastern Band of Cherokees for a longer period than any other person. First elected to the Tribal Council, he was chosen chief in 1931. He served four consecutive terms, and then was elected again in 1955 and also in 1963. The many accomplishments of Mr. Blythe for his people are a living monument to the concern and compassion he has had for them.

Jarrett was born May 30, 1886, on the Cherokee reservation in North Carolina. These Indians ran away and hid in the mountains at the time the Cherokees were being removed to Indian Territory. Since it was difficult to find them, and a costly procedure besides, they were permitted to remain and eventually the reservation was established for them. The rest of the tribe, however, went on the historic march over the "Trail of Tears."

Jarrett went to school on the reservation. Then he went to Hampton Institute in Virginia, at that time a government Indian school, and finally to Haskell Indian School in Kansas. Much of his young manhood was spent on the reservation, however.

He was a great one to trot down from his home to a flat spot of ground to get a good game of Cherokee stick ball started, or a game of baseball. The captain of his team, he was able to arrange competitive games with other teams farther away. He sometimes took his team to Whittier, some fifty miles away, going by horse and wagon to board a train for their destination.

All boy, young Jarrett sometimes had a tendency to steal eggs from a storekeeper's hen roost. These he would swap to the same storekeeper for candy or some other desired treat. The egg-stealing was a game, not an act of malice, and probably it was well known to the storekeeper, who willingly shut his eyes when he saw his own eggs coming back into the store with an engaging smile.

School days behind him, Blythe was moved by a desire to see something of the world. He went west to Montana where he spent four years working on a reclamation project. It was good to get away for a spell, but the "hang for home" never really left him. The Montana mountains were beautiful, but forbidding. At Cherokee, the mountains were soft and mystical. They were often swathed in a hazy mist which gave the Smoky Mountains their name. The Cherokee legends told that this mist came from the smoking of ghost pipes by Cherokee spirits still lingering in the highlands.

So Jarrett returned to Cherokee and was given a job with the Agricultural Extension Service, helping Cherokee people with their farming problems. He also worked for the Forestry Division in the supervision and control of the fine forested lands, and then he supervised a crew of CCC workmen on the reservation. He also had a farm of his own which he worked for many years, setting the example for others.

Because Blythe had been outside the reservation, as few

Cherokees had, and because he so involved himself with reservation concerns, he was elected to his Tribal Council position. He served with such distinction that there was no other choice for chief.

As Principal Chief, Blythe joined a long line of ancestors all noted for public service. His father was the Indian Agent at Cherokee for a number of years, and his grandfather was Principal Chief for eleven years, and Vice Chief and Secretary of the Council, also for eleven years. An uncle was Principal Chief for four years.

Married, but with no children of his own, he and his wife cared for many neglected children. He could not see a child in want or distress without doing something about it. He watched over those he took into his home and helped them to get a good start in life.

Always interested in young people, Jarrett Blythe made frequent gifts of valuable land to young couples and helped them start their homes. The "Jarrett Blythe homesteads" are scattered over the reservation.

As chief, he never failed to respond to the need of any individual Cherokee, because this is the Indian concept of what a chief should be—the servant, not the ruler, of the people. But more than this, he initiated many projects which would benefit the tribe as a whole.

For one thing, he gave the land on which a church could be built and he furnished considerable aid for its construction —this from his own resources, not from tribal funds. Once it was built, he was an active worker in the church and a regular attendant.

Because he believed that the Cherokees must have a pride in themselves and in their past, he founded the Cherokee Historical Association which maintains a museum on the reservation. The Association also constructed a reproduction of a Cherokee village as it used to be. This attracts many visitors and gives employment to Cherokee people as guides and as "residents" of the village, similar to the pattern of Williamsburg.

In line with his interest in history, Blythe was influential in starting the production of an historical drama, "Unto These Hills," which relates the story of the Cherokee people and the events which brought about the tragedy of their removal, and how it came to be that certain Cherokees remained in the Smoky Mountains.

The pageant is given nightly on the reservation during the summer months. It is produced by the drama department of the University of North Carolina and Cherokees play some of the principal parts. It is played in the Mountainside Theatre, a large amphitheatre which Jarrett Blythe also brought about.

Thousands of people see the play each year, and they go away with a completely different viewpoint and a great deal of respect for the people who suffered so much yet never gave ground.

Jarrett Blythe is not one to express opinions. He is a doer rather than a speaker, but it is obvious that these two projects —the historical association and Indian village replica, and the pageant—were born of his own deep feelings concerning his people.

"The whites don't know us, or our history," he would say. "Let us show them what we are really like." For Blythe is not hostile in his attitude toward whites. He is not going to let his people be trampled over, but he is willing to cooperate and to hold out a hand of friendship to those who will further Cherokee interests.

Tourists spend a lot of money, he observed, and there was no reason why some of it shouldn't be spent on the reservation which had much to offer. The beautiful mountains, good fishing, fine roads, the peace and quiet of the hills—these all had tourist value.

So he set about finding a way to make it possible for tourists to visit the reservation with benefit to the tribe. He proposed and helped to start construction of Boundary Tree Lodge, a luxury-type motel which is owned and operated by the tribe, and which seldom has an empty room. Here again, the motel is staffed by Cherokees, from the office to dining hall and kitchens. Later, other tribes were to follow the Cherokees in opening tourist facilities, but Blythe's was the pioneer effort.

With the new opportunities moving into the reservation, Jarrett Blythe established a loan fund available to those Indians who wanted to go into business for themselves. Indian-owned gift shops, stores, and other motels and rooming houses were soon opened with the help of this loan fund. Until then, it wasn't possible for Indians to borrow money.

Later, two industries were brought onto the reservation. One manufactures Indian style moccasins and drums, the other is a quilt manufacturing business. Again, these were pioneer efforts—the first industries to be reservation-based and to give training and employment to Cherokee workers.

Under Blythe's leadership, too, the ground was purchased by the tribe to build a modernistic, visualistic new high school, the equal of any school operated by the state.

Indian crafts also received attention. The Qualla Indian Arts and Crafts Cooperative was founded to bring back the fine handwork of the people and create a market for it.

Cherokee women now began to produce excellently made

baskets, making use of the old native materials and dyes. The Cooperative, which has a crafts center and salesroom, refused to accept any poorly made baskets and in this way stimulated the women to turning in only the best.

The Cherokees are natural woodcarvers, and so the most skilled among them were engaged to teach this art which has become an important source of revenue for the men. From this, it was an easy step to making furniture and the beautiful handmade pieces, all of native hardwoods, find ready buyers.

Jarrett Blythe preached maxims of good farming and forestry practices and initiated the annual Cherokee Fair, which is a major event in the state. Only the best of Indian-grown or Indian-made products are exhibited. He preached too, "Your people need you"—encouraging every Cherokee who could in some way be useful on the reservation to work in the cause of their own and to contribute in ways that they could.

The story of Jarrett Blythe's administration as Principal Chief is dramatic and exciting and one in which the Cherokees were helped along the road to considerable progress. From the time they had come into contact with the whites, they had been an advanced tribe, though their progress was nearly destroyed by the cruel removal and the fear of the whites which it had aroused. Snug in their mountain fastness, the Cherokees who remained in North Carolina had become ingrown and withdrawn from outside contacts.

But Blythe firmly believed that what his people had achieved at one time could be achieved again, with even better results. It needed only someone to "set the fire" and he was the spark.

Each of his terms of office was a milestone in Cherokee

history and each of his accomplishments has created ever-widening circles of good for the people.

Even though Jarrett Blythe is now retired from active service, his name and his spirit will endure in the Smoky Mountain country, and even beyond, for others were inspired by what he did. He has been called a great statesman, which he is, and he has had honors heaped upon him, among them the Indian Achievement Award. Regardless, he remains the chief of his people—the one to whom they turn for inspiration and guidance even now, the one who lives a life of service for his own with no thought of self.

Louis R. Bruce

LOUIS BRUCE, the third Indian to be Commissioner of Indian Affairs, is a member of two tribes. His father was a Mohawk and his mother a Sioux. He grew up among both people, but mainly on the Onondaga Reservation in New York State where he was born in 1906 and where his father was a Methodist minister.

Louis' father was slated to become chief of the Mohawks, as his father had been, but instead he chose to break with Indian tradition. Fond of athletics, he developed skill as a baseball player and played professionally with such teams as the Philadelphia Athletics and the New York Yankees. It was his goal to become a dentist and he paid for his dental education with his baseball earnings.

He practiced in Syracuse, but then he became associated with the Onondaga Indians and decided that he wanted to become a missionary. With his theological training completed, he was appointed pastor to the Onondaga Mission, and then spent eleven years as pastor on his home reserve, St. Regis, the Mohawk Reservation which straddles the Canadian border. To raise funds for a fine, new church, he organized an all-Mohawk male quartet which appeared in concert on numerous occasions.

Louis' grandfather, too, was a man of unusual attainment. John Bruce helped to make history in his part of the country. Many years the chief of the tribe, he journeyed often to Washington and to Albany in the interests of his people. He was also a frequent visitor to Ottawa, because the Mohawks lived both in Canada and New York.

John Bruce had much to do with the drawing up of several treaties, and he was considered a dependable person and a progressive leader. Although he spoke good English, his education was limited. He insisted, however, that his children be well educated and all six found their way to higher schools of learning.

But John Bruce is particularly noted for another piece of history.

When Lord Wolseley, leader of the British expedition attempting to rescue General Charles Gordon, who was pent up with his soldiers in Khartoum by the Moslems in 1884, he found that it would take great skill to ascend the Nile through the upper rapids. He remembered the Indians who lived along the rapids of the St. Lawrence River and who were great canoeists and boatmen.

He contacted John Bruce, and the famed Canadian "voyageurs" were organized for the rescue of Gordon. Bruce fretted at the slowness of the English in getting started and even more at the long delay in going through Egypt. He told the English commander that the Indians wanted to travel light of baggage and that in this way they could do the trip in a quarter of the time that it was taking. But the commander turned a deaf ear and held back, awaiting a full equipment of baggage. John got the British to Khartoum, but too late, for the Moslems had broken into the city and Gordon was killed.

John Bruce was given two medals by the English for his services and was taken on visits to Asia and Australia. He proudly wore his medals to the end of his life in 1931.

Louis Bruce was raised in an atmosphere of Methodist "strictness." His father ruled with a stern yet loving hand. The great battle of his life was for Indian citizenship and he campaigned on all the New York reservations in an attempt to persuade reluctant Indians to support the citizenship bill. He argued that he wanted to participate in civic affairs, and he counted as the happiest day of his life that one on which he first voted. In line with this philosophy, he gave up his ministry to the Indians and served successfully in churches in white congregations.

Young Louis was an apprehensive lad. He heard so many adverse comments about Indians that he began to feel that he belonged to a persecuted, underprivileged group.

This his father refused to countenance. "You must stop being disturbed about being an Indian," he told his son. "In this country, everything will depend on what you make of yourself, and you will have just exactly as much opportunity as the next person. Your obstacles are mainly in your own mind."

But still Louis was bothered by what he heard. From his white neighbors, he heard that Indians were "no-good trash," yet he had good friends among the whites. From the Indians, he heard of the raw deal they had been given since the whites arrived in America. He heard that it was hopeless for an Indian to try to improve his position because of the deep prejudice against them.

And he came to know better, and to prove better, on both

counts. He made it a point to inform people immediately of his Indian blood to avoid any embarrassing remarks, and he found that he was treated as any other person. But for a long time he suffered from the inferiority complex which so many Indians have. "If it were not for my father and the stern stuff of which he was made, I would have remained on the reservation," Louis says.

The Bruces were never well off financially. Reverend Bruce rarely earned more than $600 a year in his early ministry. Because he understood the sufferings of his son, he decided to take drastic action—to throw him into the American stream of life, to sink or swim. Able to get a reduction in tuition at Cazenovia Seminary, a Methodist school, he enrolled the boy there.

In his first weeks at Cazenovia, Louis Bruce was terribly conscious of being watched. The three hundred students had never seen an Indian before and they expected him to dress and talk like they supposed Indians talked—with an ugh! here and an ugh! there. His parents were watching too, and so were the Indians on the reservation who expected that he would either be thrown out of school, or return of his own volition.

"If I had failed, no doubt I would have crawled back into my shell," Bruce says. "But happily, the lessons my father drilled into me paid off. I became captain of Cazenovia's football, basketball, and track teams, and president of my senior class."

At Cazenovia, Louis played the male lead in the junior class play. The leading lady was a white girl, the daughter of a Cornell-educated farmer. The two went on to Syracuse University together where Louis earned his way by working as a hired hand on her father's farm.

The months at school were touch-and-go financially. He waited on tables, mowed lawns, dug postholes, cracked rock, wrestled logs at a paper pulp mill, operated a pick and shovel. He never went to a football game, because he had to work on Saturdays. He was Syracuse's star pole vaulter but was never able to go on an out-of-town trip with the team, because he had to earn money.

At college, Bruce majored in psychology, hoping to help himself with his inferiority feelings and to understand them better. The hardest thing for an Indian to become is aggressive, to sell himself, and Louis had all of the Indian reticence and diffidence. Whatever he decided to do as a vocation, he had first to prove to himself that he could make good in the American way.

He decided that Americans are the greatest salesmen on earth and he set out, grimly, to become a salesman. He signed up for merchandising courses, got a spare-time job selling men's clothing on commission, and practiced putting himself across each night in front of a mirror.

But at the store, each customer still looked like a glowering monster. He would clench his fists and force himself to go forward, grinning his most practiced smile and feeling ridiculous. In his third week he managed to sell a $60 suit to a man who wanted to spend only $35, and was convinced that he could sell after all.

He graduated from college in the year of the Great Depression. College graduates were a nickel a dozen, and Indian college graduates, of which there were very few, were not even that. When he heard of an opening with a men's clothing store in New York City, he borrowed train fare and hurried down and got the job in the face of many graduates from the big colleges such as Harvard and Princeton. He knew the men's clothing business from experience, and he could discuss it with intelligence.

Married now to the girl of his school days, he brought his wife to the city and she worked in a department store. The couple got along well, and Louis was soon a department head with five assistants. Actually, his heart was not in a business career, though. He was still "too Indian" to be interested in making money. Closer to his heart was the plight of Indian children on the reservations with absolutely nothing to encourage them. They were completely demoralized and more ashamed of their Indian blood than ever.

Suddenly, he got a brain storm. There were thousands of camps in the New England-New York area, most of them with Indian programs and not one with a real Indian teaching them. He hurried to the Onondaga Reservation and presented a plan to the chiefs for Indians to teach Indian lore in camps. At first, enthusiasm ran high—then all was gloom again. Indian youngsters were not interested in their background and would have to be trained in it—if they were willing to be trained.

Then Louis made another proposal. The government was spending millions of dollars for "leaf-raking projects" through the WPA and Louis felt that the idea to provide work for people was a good one. His plan with regard to summer camps would give Indian young people constructive work if he could convince the government to finance the program and summer camps to hire Indian counselors. He quit his job and went to work selling the idea to both the government and the camps, and in five years he helped to put six hundred Indian boys on camp staffs where they made good money and began to take pride in their Indian heritage.

Several hundred of these young people resumed their high

school educations and many went back to college. When federal funds were finally withdrawn, New York reservations still continued to provide Indian camp counselors.

With the program well established, and with two children of his own, Louis now felt the need to get back to the land. He wanted to settle down in a small community and sink roots. He wanted to succeed in such a community in the way his father had done all of his life—by serving people. He wanted to become a farmer.

It was then that his father-in-law announced that he wanted to withdraw gradually from the management of his fine dairy farm. Louis was in the farming business and, in a few years, he added an additional 160-acre farm to the several hundred acres.

He was "up to his ears" in community activities—Boy Scouts, PTA, and church work—in the nearby town of Richfield Springs when he noticed that the young people were steadily leaving. They had the same discouraging problem that faced the reservation youngsters. There was nothing to do—the town was dead, there was nothing to hold them.

Louis then began to hold meetings in his home, focusing on the theme "Does Our Town Have a Future?" The young people inspired many new ideas and new industries were brought in and some of the youngsters became top leaders in the community.

But rural youth, too, needed attention. Louis Bruce became a member of the Dairymen's League Cooperative Association for which he developed an active youth program in the county. He spent much time in travel in connection with this program. His children—now two boys and a girl—were taught to shoulder responsibility for the farm. They had regular chores—feeding the calves, driving the cows to pasture, gathering eggs, throwing down the hay, weeding the vegetables, and doing the milking. One of these sons now manages the Bruce farm today. The other is a distinguished physicist.

Bruce's interest in young people has been an abiding one. When he became president of the Dairymen's League he organized young farm people in communities and, as Youth Director, he supervised the only program of its kind in the country. Under his leadership, the first National American Indian Youth Conference was held in Washington, and he has brought many young people into key positions in the Bureau of Indian Affairs since he was appointed Commissioner.

In 1949, Louis submitted an article, "What America Means to Me," to *American* magazine. It was published and reprinted in the *Reader's Digest* in sixteen languages throughout the world. It brought him a Freedom Foundation Award, and this, with his other fine achievements, won him the Indian Achievement Award.

Before he became Commissioner of Indian Affairs, Louis rounded out his career as an executive for a national advertising agency, as special assistant commissioner for cooperative housing in the Federal Housing Administration, as public relations director for a chain of twenty-three cooperative supermarkets, and as executive director and chairman of the Board of Trustees, Zeta Psi Educational Foundation. In his position with the FHA, he promoted and organized the first National American Indian Conference on Housing.

When Louis Bruce became Commissioner, he stated that it was his intent to make the Indian Bureau fully responsive to the needs and direction of Indian people and supportive of their efforts and decisions.

"I will help the Indians put the Bureau programs together

as they want them, not dictate the terms," he said. "The way to Indian progress is involvement in opportunity; it is up to Indians how to arrange this. For many years we have been hearing about the plight of the Indian. We have been fighting statistics which indicate Indians have the lowest standard of living. We have been pitied and we have been neglected. But I want to speak of might. We, as a people, have been making progress because we are accepting challenges with a new energy and a new confidence and we are witnessing a rebirth of Indian spirit and determination."

He pledged that he would turn the BIA into a service rather than a management organization, and he proceeded to establish a huge house-cleaning which both shocked and startled Indians and government employees alike—and which is still having repercussions. The new program was based on what Indians said they wanted and, within memory, no such sweeping changes have ever taken place within the hierarchy of the Bureau.

One of the first acts was to establish an entirely new structure with new departments and new functions. "I want to get Indians fully involved in decisions affecting them," Louis Bruce says. "Indians are to be full partners in discussing, planning, and implementing programs and services to improve all facets of their lives."

Since he has been Commissioner, more and more programs have been started fully operated by Indians. One tribe, the Zuni, has taken over the complete management of its reservation, and Indian communities have taken over the management of Indian schools.

"I want to see Indians buying cars from Indians on reservations, and buying food in Indian-owned stores, driving on Indian-planned and Indian-built roads, talking on Indian-owned telephone systems, and living in an Indian-managed economy," Mr. Bruce states in discussing his plans for the future. "Indian economy can be as stable as any other economy when the dollars can be exchanged numerous times in the local community. It is up to Indians to take the bull by the horns if they wish. My office stands ready to cooperate, to travel a new road in Indian affairs so that meaningful and positive gains are made for the economical and social development of Indian country."

Leon Cook

THE meeting hall in Reno was in a tumult. During the week, the National Congress of American Indians, the country's largest organization of Indians, had been assembled in convention, the most turbulent in their history. The Congress had been feeling the growing pains of sharp conflicts between reservation and urban Indians and of the need to establish a common front on issues facing Indian people.

Suddenly the room was hushed. It was almost as though the people had stopped breathing. The results of the presidential election were to be announced and here, again, tensions had run high. There had been a number of candidates, each with their ardent followers.

The election chairman stepped to the fore and read the verdict. Leon Cook by a large majority! The noise and the pounding of drums almost brought the walls down.

Leon Cook is the youngest man to hold the presidency of this group, the oldest all-Indian organization. He was also the first Indian not identified as a tribal chairman to be elected to the office.

He comes from the Red Lake Chippewa Reservation in Minnesota, although his great-great-grandmother was a

Sioux. She was either left behind when her people moved, or was captured by the Chippewa and raised by them. Her son was Amos Bigbird who was a recognized Chippewa chief and Leon's great-grandfather.

"I've been without a family much of my life," Leon says. "My mother died shortly after I was born in 1939, and my father was killed in an auto accident when I was seven years old. My sister and I were raised by relatives until we both went away to school."

Before this, Leon completed grade school on the reservation. "I was the best paper boy the Red Lake Reservation ever had," he reminisces. "Without a family, it was necessary for me to work and I did so every day after school, on weekends, and throughout the summer for a local grocery store."

An enterprising lad, Leon saved his money, and started a number of "private contracts" for himself—everything from cutting wood, hauling waste, and mowing lawns. His paper route had ninety customers, and he consistently made the weekly honor role for paying his bills to the newspaper.

While he was still in eighth grade, Leon was taken on a visit to St. John's Abbey Prep School. The visit fired his interest and he thought there could be nothing finer than to go to a school like that. The young boy so eager to attend school met with a reciprocal interest at St. John's. He was offered a scholarship to cover half of his expenses. Leon paid the rest with the $500 he had managed to save from his various jobs and "contracts." "Incidentally," he laughs, "I don't think I've saved that amount of money since."

School was a delight and by the time he graduated from high school he had talked himself into going to college. "I couldn't take the pressure of my peers," Leon recalls. "They were all talking about where they were going in their junior year, and I hadn't even thought about *if* I was going. It had been tough enough to finance my way through high school."

With the decision made to continue schooling, Leon elected to remain at St. John's where he had been quite happy, and to enroll in their college division. The college years were exciting and enjoyable, but he dropped out in the second semester when he became a senior.

"I guess it was a combination of 'senioritis' and poor money management that led to this," he explains. "I was just too exhausted to continue."

While this could have been a tragedy, Leon found that it led to a healthy and profitable experience. Two years later he returned to finish the one uncompleted semester, but in the meantime he became the owner-operator of a structural restoration company.

He married, and "rediscovered" himself. He also found that he had an enduring interest in his own people even though he was living away from them.

"I realized for the first time how fortunate I had been," he says. "I had struggled through life on the reservation, struggled through school and college, and had never really taken time to look at my background and people. They were just there, and I was just one of them—but not really one of them. I was too busy scrounging to keep myself going."

In one of his college courses, Leon had read about settlement houses. He discovered that the Waite Neighborhood House in Minneapolis had a worker who was an Indian, and another Indian as Program Director. They had a large clientele of city Indians with all kinds of problems. Even the two Indian workers had problems over being Indians.

"To me, this was nothing short of surprising," Leon says. "Looking back, I knew that I had always been happy and proud to be Indian. I had never come up against racial prejudice and most people I met were pleased to have an Indian as friend or 'buddy.' "

Out of his childhood, he remembered an incident that took place when he was ten years old. He lived in Sterling, Illinois, with one of his father's sisters. Sterling is an industrial city with a large Mexican population, and one day, in the grocery store, the clerk called Leon a *muchacho*. When he learned that the boy was Indian, not Mexican, he introduced him with much enthusiasm to all the customers and insisted that he meet his father, also.

The clerk's father was a national roller skating champion. He took such a liking to Leon that he took him to a roller derby in Chicago as his Indian friend.

Leon made many other friends in Sterling, and even had his portrait painted by artists, "all because I was an Indian."

"Every experience was a positive one and reinforced my pride in being Indian, and this continued throughout all of my schooling and in everything else I've ever done," Leon says now.

Comparing his own experiences with the attitudes expressed by the city Indians whom he contacted, Leon decided to go to graduate school in the School of Social Work at the University of Minnesota. He gave up his work, which was mainly "steeple-jacking" and studied group work and community organization, working at Waite House in off-hours as Indian Services Director. In the summer, he returned to being a steeple jack and construction worker tuck-pointer.

His last year in graduate school became a hectic one. Invited to serve on the board of directors of the Mille Lacs Foundation, he became involved in the fund-raising activity for the Mille Lacs Reservation. As a result of the cooperation between the tribe and the Foundation, Mille Lacs has probably one of the most impressive success stories of any reservation in the country.

While he was still in graduate school, Leon decided to run for the office of Tribal Chairman at Red Lake. "I most certainly didn't come out the winner," he laughs. "I soothed my ego by thinking that I may have lost the battle, but I had really won the war. Nevertheless, I would much rather have won the battle."

In his first nine months out of school, Leon worked as director of VISTA (Volunteers in Service to America), Minneapolis, and OEO (Office of Economic Opportunity), Minneapolis and Duluth. He was director of the VISTA training center in a program geared to providing training for working in urban areas.

"How about that?" Leon asks. "I have a feeling that nobody ever saw the humor of it all except me—an Indian from the sticks training blacks and Anglos for working in the city!"

Moving over to the Minneapolis OEO program, Leon was a consultant to the Director and he performed the groundwork that eventually led to the establishment of the Minneapolis Indian Center. In Duluth, he set up and operated the Neighborhood Youth Corps.

His next move was to the EDA (Economic Development Administration) Duluth office. While here, he was offered the position of Field Coordinator for the states of Arizona and Nevada, primarily because most of the areas eligible for assistance were Indian reservations.

"This was really Indian country. My people, the Chippewa, are sometimes called the 'smoked Swedes.' There is little of Indian identification about us. But with EDA I had to learn all kinds of new tribal names and far different surnames. Chippewas and Sioux are one thing; Hualapais, Yavapais, Shoshones, Chemehuevis are something else again."

Throwing himself into this work, Leon was provided with exposure to such a wide variety of tribes and reservations that the so-called "Indian experts and the anthropologists would have been totally overwhelmed by it all," he says. "One thing, the problems and the circumstances facing the Indians in the Southwest are no different than anywhere else in the country."

Now Leon was asked to join the Bureau of Indian Affairs in a key position, one of the young leaders that the Commissioner was hoping to bring in as a team. It was a tempting offer, but Leon had to wrestle with himself.

"I found myself in the throes of ambivalence," he remarks. "I had criticized the BIA most of my life. Now I was confronted with the challenge to help do something about it. The anxieties piled up. I had many friends and comrades in Indian country and elsewhere and I wanted to hold fast to them. But it was clearly demonstrated in the past that an Indian in the BIA often wound up with more enemies than friends. I didn't want to be a cop-out, but I didn't want to be a sell-out, either. The crux of my anxiety was that I would rather try than not try at all. This has been my philosophy in life, and when I finally said that I would go with the BIA, I hoped that the Great Spirit would lead me in the right path."

In the Bureau of Indian Affairs, Leon was in the second highest spot in the economic division. With a grasp of resource issues and their defense, and a knowledge of business procedures and funding, he soon made "his presence felt."

For one thing, he turned Indian water rights into a *cause*

célèbre among Indians and a nightmare for the White House. But his tough-talking differences over policies caused him to resign from the Bureau in order to "maintain my self-respect." He strongly felt that the team of younger Indians should be given the responsibility the Commissioner wanted them to have, and this was being circumvented by old-line employees, he charged.

With his resignation, Leon had become something of a national figure. Calling himself an "activist" and favoring militancy so long as it was constructive, Leon embarked on a plea for Indian unity at the NCAI convention. Possessed of a great deal of personal charm, and a way of making "impact" points, he wound up as the new president.

Since Leon assumed office, the National Congress has entered into an unprecedented coalition with several other Indian organizations. The new group—the Coalition of Organized Indians and Natives (COINS)—will establish a common front on issues facing the nation's Indian people and will fashion common political strategies. Among other activities, this joint national effort, bridging the sometimes anguished breach between reservation and city Indians, is viewed as historic in nature.

Says Leon Cook, who was influential in bringing it about: "The coalition . . . will represent the Indian world at this point in time . . . It is proof positive that we can—as we must —be genuinely together."

Vine Deloria, Jr.

At a conference held in New York City between non-Indian leaders of various groups concerned with Indian rights and welfare, a handsome young Indian rose to his feet. He discussed the matters at hand with a piece of biting wit: "After all, Custer died for *your* sins."

Although spoken in half-jest, these words were to become a slogan and a battle cry among youthful Indians. They were printed on bumper stickers, on stationery, on hat bands and badges, or flaunted in every other possible way. They became the title of the speaker's first book which rocketed to the best-selling lists and to a number of printings.

Vine Deloria, Jr., the originator of the phrase, is a Yankton Sioux or Dakota. He was born in South Dakota in 1934 to a distinguished Indian family of scholars, churchmen, and warrior chief ancestors.

His great-great-grandfather, Phillipe Des Lauriers, came to America as a child after his parents were guillotined during the French Revolution. When Des Lauriers was grown, he became a fur trader and married the daughter of a Yankton chief. Their son was a prominent warrior, and his son,

56

Vine's grandfather, was one of the first Indian converts to the Episcopalian faith.

This grandfather, whose Indian name was Tipi Sapa, changed his name to Philip Deloria, Anglicizing the original French name. He spent forty years as an ordained priest among his people and he brought hundreds of Sioux into the Christian religion. He established twelve Indian chapels in Dakota Territory.

Philip Deloria is depicted among nearly ninety sculptured figures which form the "company of heaven"—prophets, apostles, martyrs, and other historical characters surrounding "Christ in Majesty" in the Episcopal National Cathedral in Washington.

Vine's father, Vine Deloria, Sr., also entered the ministry, inspired by his father's example. He spent thirty-seven years as a missionary among the Sioux and for a number of years was Assistant Secretary in the Division of Domestic Missions on the National Council staff of the church. He was the first Indian in history to hold a national executive post in the Episcopal faith. Before his retirement, he had become archdeacon of the Niobrara Deaconry, working among the Indians of South Dakota.

Ella, a daughter of Philip and Vine's aunt, became a noteworthy anthropologist and an authority on the customs and culture of the Sioux.

It was Vine's people who were among the bands of Sioux who wiped out General Custer and his troops at the Battle of the Little Big Horn. So the memory of Custer and of what took place was a vivid one, for survivors of that terrible happening still lived among the older Sioux.

When Vine was a year old, the Indian Reorganization Act was passed. This was landmark legislation, since it allowed

Indian tribes for the first time the full rights of self-govern-ment. Until then, Indians had little voice in the decisions that were made which affected their lives and their prop-erties. Indian religious ceremonies had been forbidden, In-dian customs were being stamped out, and even tribal lan-guage was not permitted to be spoken in Indian schools.

"Indians must become like white people" was the philoso-phy of the time, and there were rigid practices put into effect to bring this about without respect to Indian feelings in the matter. In the early reservation years, the Sioux were not given their food rations until the men agreed to farm the small acreages allotted to each family. But these were a hunting people, roamers of the Plains and proud warriors. For men to farm was to them a disgrace. Farming was against their very natures.

Many of the Sioux did become prosperous ranchers, how-ever. But with World War I, their cattle was sold by the government for war needs, and at the war's end, the land was leased to whites. This made the white ranchers wealthy, and the Indians destitute lease-holders.

With the Indian Reorganization Act, there was a reversal of policy. There was no prohibition of Indian religious cere-monies or of Indian custom. Indeed, there was an encourage-ment of turning back to those things that were meaningful.

As an infant, Vine was taken on trips to attend the Indian dances, now, with the new situation, in full swing. From everywhere the people gathered, coming by team and wagon and traversing the terrible, rutted roads or the rough land where there were no roads at all.

The dances were great emotional events in which the people rejoiced with fervor. This was something of their own now restored to them and which had always been held

in their hearts. Warriors who had fought in the Custer battle, who had been afraid to speak of their part in what had
taken place, now recited their acts of bravery and counted
the honors that had been theirs.

Of all of Vine's childhood memories, the one that stands
first and foremost was a visit to the site of Wounded Knee
where two hundred Sioux, men, women and children, were
slain by a troop of Cavalry, in retaliation for what had happened to Custer, the Indians have always believed. The
episode was so terrible that it left an unerasable scar on every
Sioux heart, and a huge black mark on the pages of American
Indian history.

Vine's father would often point out to him people who
had lived through the massacre, and explain to his son why
all of the people went out of their way to help them. Helping was an obligation that no one would shirk.

Even though Vine's father was a priest and dedicated to
Christian service, he still had roots deep in Indian ways
which were very much a part of his own childhood. He was
strongly responsive to the side of him that was Indian, and
often strongly questioning of the program of the church.
Young Vine, as he grew up on the reservation and witnessed
the many problems of his people in a wide panorama of
frustration, unrest, and change, could not help but be affected
by this same inner conflict.

It was his intent to maintain the family tradition and become a priest like his father and grandfather before him, so
he left the reservation in 1951, attended college at Iowa State
University, served in the Marines, and then enrolled for
seminary training.

When he graduated he was employed by the United
Scholarship Service, a church-founded group devoted to

assisting Indian and Mexican students to obtain secondary school and college education. Because he had spent the last two years of his schooling in an eastern preparatory school—probably the only Indian in his age bracket to have done so—he was placed in charge of developing the placement of Indian students in such schools.

This was a pioneer venture, and Vine insisted that all of the students involved be qualified for scholarships as students and not as Indians.

"It seemed to me that this was the only way for Indians to gain the white man's respect," Vine says. "I didn't think we should cry our way into schools; that kind of sympathy would destroy the students we were trying to help."

But the people who were supporting the program saw it differently. They wanted to continue the customary soft-hearted paternalism toward Indians and they accused Deloria of trying to form an "elite" group of above-average intellectual and academic abilities.

Refusing to change the opinions that he felt with all of his being, Vine Deloria began to have his first doubts of the attitudes and objectives of the church. He veered away from continuing religious education and accepted the position of executive secretary of the National Congress of American Indians. This was to be a proving ground, for he now came into immediate contact with tribes throughout the country.

"I learned more in my three years with the NCAI than I had in the previous thirty years of my life," he says. "Every conceivable problem that could occur in an Indian society was suddenly thrust at me from 315 different tribal directions. I discovered that I was expected to solve these problems and I found that Indian people locally and on the national level were being played against each other by unscrupulous individuals with ego or income at stake. There were solutions, but few could be successfully put into effect or even tried because of those who worked night and day to destroy the unity we were seeking as a people."

A whole generation of young people who had grown up after World War II had left the reservations and gotten educations. They were returning now as "educated Indians" who thought they could improve matters, but somehow tribal groups were strangely resistant to their ideas. The tribes had existed for centuries without going outside for education and information, and leadership was still the province of the elderly and not of the young. Those with an education were often accused of being "white Indians"—no longer at home or a part of Indian culture. "You think white" sent many a young Indian aspirant down to crushing humiliation.

As executive secretary of the NCAI, Deloria made the rounds of the conference circuit, attending numerous meetings, meeting with tribal councils, working with government agencies and programs, raising funds for the organization, and developing plans and projects, legislative action, and other activities that were organization-sponsored.

In spite of all of his effort, he found that the reservation people went pretty much their own way, even so, "plodding along on their own time schedule and doing what they considered to be important without regard to the advice of the young 'Indian experts.' "

Discouragement set in. Conferences were proving unproductive, and "where non-Indians had been pushed out to make room for Indians, they had managed to regain control of the major programs serving Indians. Indian administrators had been pushed aside."

With other young leaders, Vine Deloria began to work

at local levels to build community movements from the ground up, for the reservation people were making steady progress. By consolidating local organizations, it was felt that greater influence could be brought to bear on national thinking.

The strong regional organizations were favored, and the NCAI continued, also, to grow. But another factor emerged —these were the young Indians who had been trained in the old ways of thought and life, and who had now become a major force in the whole Indian community.

It was apparent to Vine that an Indian revolution was well under way and that it was complicated by several factions— the NCAI, which represented the modern, contemporary Indian through tribal governments; the activists who were willing to copy black militant tactics; and the traditionalists who demanded a return to basic Indian philosophy and a complete revival of Indian ways and forms of government.

Therefore, Vine did not continue his NCAI position, but entered law school at the University of Colorado instead. He felt that a good legal education would be needed in order to have an Indian legal program for the defense of Indian treaty rights.

With him setting the example, it was not long before nearly fifty other young Indians entered law schools with the help of the Ford Foundation. There will be no lack of legal talent for Indians in the years ahead, and this talent will be comprised of Indians who are dedicated to Indian interests and determined to right the injustices that have taken place. More and more Indians are turning to law studies, many inspired by Vine Deloria.

While he was in law school, Vine wrote his first book, *Custer Died for Your Sins,* a brilliant treatise. It sets the records straight, smashes the stereotypes, myths, and half-truths persisting in the public mind, and states in no uncertain terms what Indians want for themselves.

Vine's anger over the exploitation of his people is apparent, as is his pride in being Indian. There is evidence of bitterness, too, although it is held on a leash, but there is no complaint about a denial of integration into white society. He says, rather, that integration is a major problem foisted on Indians by the white man in an effort to force him to accept white values for which he has contempt.

For this reason, Vine says, Indians have not been able to understand the quest of the blacks for integration into a white society with nothing to offer but white culture which is "not really a culture but a cancer."

His advice to blacks has been to drop the façade of integration. "Be yourself and you'll get the backing of the exploited Indian, who'll finally understand you and believe you understand him."

With regard to integration, Vine offers this paradox: "In order to keep the country from complete divisiveness, separatism must be accepted as a means to achieve equality of personality both for groups and individuals.

"Separatism can be the means by which blacks gain time for reflection, meditation, and eventual understanding of themselves as a people."

Indians could not identify with black problems, Vine explains, because blacks did not, until recently, seem to sense their salvation in respect for their own mores. He thinks, however, that Indians will be able to join with blacks in an alliance of oppressed but dissimilar minority groups, if black militancy leads to "nationalistic philosophies which relate to the ongoing conception of the tribe as a nation extending in time and occupying space."

At no time does Vine advocate violence for overcoming problems. He says that ideological leverage is always superior to physical force. He also counsels that there must be unity of thought and action, for "Indians, themselves, weaken efforts to develop effective working relationships between tribes because of intense rivalries, jealousies, and a liking for playing politics.

"Indians do not need someone to study us, feel sorry for us, identify with us, or claim descent from Pocahontas to make us feel better," Vine states forthrightly. "Nor do we need to be classified as semi-white and have programs made to bleach us further . . . we need . . . a new policy from Congress that acknowledges our new intelligence and our dignity."

With the success of his first book, Vine's second was soon under way. This is titled *We Talk, You Listen*. A third book, *Utmost Good Faith*, appeared in a short while. Like the first, these two are directly related to Indian people. They are basically a protest against paternalism of groups "dominated by whites and do-gooders who do more harm than good."

When asked about his books, Vine says, "They are liked in the East because Easterners are not near Indians. They are disliked in the West because Westerners are trying to get Indian lands and therefore they would not like my books."

Because of their treaty rights, Indians are different from other minority groups, Vine says, and treaty and aboriginal rights must be firmly established.

Indians would lose a great deal if they were integrated without the protection of their treaty rights, for there are special privileges and benefits accruing to them under this relationship with the government which are not given to any other people.

Indians, for example, do not pay taxes on their held-in-trust lands. They are provided with schooling and with health and hospital care and with administrative services for their property.

Many programs that have been established for Indians have caused a leadership upheaval which is nurtured by the opportunities created. Many capable young leaders have seemed to rise from nowhere, Vine says.

"Indian leadership has waited and planned for the day when these opportunities for more and creative self-government would arise."

At the same time, a twentieth-century "Indianism" has also arisen in which younger Indians feel a nationalistic responsibility to work for their tribes, and many times this is not based on a reservation background or upbringing, it is pointed out.

"The more educated Indians become the more they seem to hold fast to tribal values; the more they base their philosophies in the survival of the tribe; and the more they seem to detect the social flaws of the American mainstream."

The philosophy of the American mainstream has been that "some will make it and some won't," Vine says. There is too large a percentage of those who won't and the losers gather to take by force what they have been denied.

"Perhaps the mainstream is the problem rather than the disadvantaged people it has created."

Any failure to recognize Indian leadership will only frustrate all attempts to solve problems, Vine emphasizes, and

"Indian leadership should be provided with the tools to create the future."

A trail blazer throughout his life, Vine now heads another pioneer venture for Indians. This is the Institute for the Development of Indian Law, which has been formed to deal exclusively with Indian legal issues.

In accepting this position, Vine commented: "We need to make apparent problems of land grabs and resource grabs which did not end with the conquest of the frontier, for they are still going on. We want to recognize and continue tribal diversity in legal terms acceptable to the tribes themselves, founded on their traditions. By defining diversity we're challenging the nation to live up to the ideas of its Constitution."

The Institute publishes a scholarly Indian law journal for experts, provides a legal indoctrination information service for tribes and Indian organizations, and prepares in-depth periodic reports on legal aspects of Indian affairs. It will pursue actual litigation in selected cases, train Indian law students, and publish a jurisprudence textbook which will contain a total theory of Indian law.

And so Vine Deloria's life has taken shape with a direction and purpose that is bound to also shape Indian directions importantly and with far-reaching results in the Indians' favor.

He firmly believes that tribalism is a viable political force and form with which to meet the modern world. It is his opinion that Indians will re-tribalize, re-colonize, and re-customize; that they are capable of, and will recreate, a type of society which can defy, mystify, and educate the rest of society.

"Indians will survive," he says, "because we are a people

unified by our humanity, not a pressure group unified for conquest."

Indian people have managed to maintain a flexible and cohesive social order in spite of everything that non-Indians have thrown at them in an attempt to break down tribal structure. At the same time, Vine says, the non-Indian society has created a monstrosity of a culture where people starve with the granaries filled, and the sun has trouble breaking through the smog.

This still young man, with a sagacity beyond his years, reiterates that ancient tribalism can be equated with modern technology in an urban setting. "It just seems to a lot of Indians that this continent was a lot better off when we were running it," he says.

Archie Demmert

ARCHIE DEMMERT stands high in his chosen career of teacher. It is said of him that "no Alaskan has added more to the quality and length of schooling among Alaskan natives," and, "many Alaskan Indians who finished college or who hold higher degrees are in some way indebted to him."

His own battle for an education was tough and uphill, and his life story is one of exceptional determination and fortitude.

Archie was born on a boat at sea a few miles north of Prince of Wales Island in 1909. His parents were Tlingit Indians, his father a salmon fisherman.

The Tlingits are one of the most unusual Indian groups in America. Originally, they lived in British Columbia, and they are one of the most important tribes of the Northwest Coast culture, one of the most unique among Indians.

A Tlingit village was made up of huge plank houses riven from the giant trees that grew along the coast. The sea-going boats in which the Tlingits hunted the salmon, halibut, seals, and sea otters were also made from these trees, as were the totem poles that stood before each house like tall history books, for they were records of the family lineage.

Everything was elaborately carved in distinctive bold designs, unlike anything seen elsewhere. There was no item too small to be intricately carved, and there was no item without this carving. Yet, the Indians were without tools of any kind other than primitive knives, and they had no mechanical devices, not even a simple pulley. Yet, they were masters at carving and at cutting down and moving the tremendous cedar trees to shape the wood as they wished.

The Tlingits did no hunting other than that of the sea, and they practiced no agriculture. The dense forests and the rocky coastland did not permit this. They were traders, however, and exchanged blankets woven of goat hair, baskets made from cedar, and the oolichan fish were so rich in oil they were burned as candles to light the enormous houses.

The houses could hold as many as two hundred or more people, and they were occupied by a large number of families. Strange ceremonies were held in the houses and dramatic pageants with masked actors portraying characters in ancient stories were held frequently.

At such events, a chief would give away all that he possessed in order to establish his status as a person of wealth, but actually he gave away nothing because everything given had to be returned to him at double interest at the next year's ceremonial feast. To be deeply in debt was an honor rather than an embarrassment, and something much to be desired.

The cultural pattern also included a rigid caste system of nobles and commoners and the ownership of slaves. Slave-raiding parties roamed the coast and those taken captive were the absolute possession of the man who captured them. They had no human rights or standing and could be put to death at the whim of their owner.

When trading vessels came among the Northwest Coast

Indians in search of the valuable furs, the Indian way of life was completely demoralized. The Tlingits, a warlike people, did not knuckle down to the Russians, who became dominant in their area and who inflicted great suffering on the people. Finally, they moved to Alaska, where, under the influence of missionaries, they gave up their old ways, for the most part, though sea fishing remained an occupation.

The clan-caste system was preserved, and Archie Demmert was born into the Raven Clan, one of the highest in the tribe.

On land, the Demmert family lived in the little Indian village of Klawock in southern Alaska. Archie grew up with the scent of the sea and the salmon in his nostrils and the roar of the waves in his ears, like the pounding of Tlingit ceremonial drums. He would wonder about the old days, at times, and what it was like when the Indians lived "as Indians." Almost, he could see the mythical beings that were part of those older memories.

An Indian boy learns early to become skilled in the tasks that he will perform as a man, and Archie was no exception to this practice. He was helping to mend nets and other fishing gear when he was still quite small, and he was as at home on the fishing boats as he was on land.

He went to school in his home village until he was old enough to go away to a government boarding school for Indians in Oregon. How different it was from his rugged Alaska! At the school, he was a student teacher in the machine shop for two years before he graduated. From this experience, he found that he liked to teach and, with this in mind, he continued his education for two years at Western Washington College.

His plan was to return to Klawock and teach in the school

there, at the same time helping his father with his salmon cannery operation. The plan was carried out, but Archie was not satisfied for long. When an opportunity came along to develop and own a general mercantile store, Archie latched on to it. He operated the store until the beginning of World War II.

Enlisting in the Army, Archie served in the Pacific Theater. It was then, he says, that he decided he wanted to be a full-time educator.

"It takes an education to be a leader," he observed, "and with an education every follower can become a leader in some way, or, a leader can advance in continual service."

Upon his discharge from the Army, Archie taught for a while in Alaska. Then with his GI money and with what he had saved from his salary, he enrolled at Wisconsin State University to secure his bachelor's degree in education.

Before he completed his sophomore year, a terrible blow fell. This was the death of his wife, which left him with two small daughters to care for. It became increasingly difficult to complete his studies, but complete them he did, when he was forty-four years old. The men who fish the sea are a hardy people and they are able to endure great hardship. Archie endured this time of great sorrow and he also remained spiritually strong.

With his degree accomplished, Archie could have remained as a teacher in Wisconsin, but his interests lay with his people in his native Alaska. It was for them that he had gotten his education. There were far too many Indian, Eskimo, and Aleut children who were not getting sufficient schooling and these children were, to him, a primary concern.

He returned to Alaska to teach in the village of Angoon. The years spent there were challenging and rewarding.

"I learned," Archie says, "that all students are different and none are typical. Some will go slowly, some will go rapidly, and others will appear to go around in circles. Let each work at his own pace and each will reach his own goal."

A gentle person, but nevertheless a man of iron will and determination, Archie held each student to the line and maintained strong but benevolent discipline. Indian children are never punished, but are always shown why an action is wrong and made to understand that it is not to be repeated. Explanation was the key to training, rather than inflicting pain, and Archie applied much of this philosophy in his relations with his students.

Then, he was asked to return to Klawock. The Tlingits were building a new school and Archie was needed to organize the program. He stayed at Klawock until the school was in full operation.

From Klawock he moved to Kake, a Haida Indian town with a growing school population. Archie was instrumental in organizing the high school for the Haida people.

But school administration took him too much away from the classroom, and it was the direct contact with the students that he loved.

"To be an effective teacher, I must give my full attention to my pupils and their studies," he decided.

So, he accepted an offer to teach in the Sitka school system. In the summers, he completed the work for his Master's degree at the University of Alaska and received this when he was fifty-five.

A teacher must not only teach, but must motivate, Archie Demmert says. "A teacher must be a living inspiration to his students so that they will continue their education—he must direct and assist them to choose a field in which their talents will be the most useful."

A man of eloquent silences and brilliant insight, Archie was not one to express an opinion without putting it into action.

"In more than forty years of teaching in many parts of Alaska," he says, "I urged, aided, persuaded, and, yes, even deviled hundreds of native youngsters to go to school, stay in school, and continue their higher schooling.

"As Indians and Eskimos move ahead the great need is for educated people who can represent them in dealings with both the state and federal governments, and for those that can fill higher positions on an equal basis with anyone else in the state. We are native Alaskan people and as such we should be fully participating in the affairs of our homeland."

The rightness of this thinking was apparent in the recent settlement of the Alaskan Native Claims Bill in Congress. The presentation and handling of this extremely important measure by the young, educated native men, both Indian and Eskimo, was historically significant and a bright star in the record of native-white relations. These who furthered the Bill won high praise in both the House and Senate.

Archie continued on his warm, quiet, and dignified teaching way. His classes were orderly, though informal. His students moved freely and took part actively, and they listened with rapt attention—whether Indian or white—to the Tlingit stories that he told as a special treat. Everyone worked hard, for Archie held them to a high standard.

"My students keep me teaching," he said. "They keep me on my toes and I learn a lot from them."

His own children were encouraged to become teachers. Both of his daughters entered the teaching field and both attended Wisconsin State University where Archie, himself, had started.

In 1969, Mr. Demmert was named to the National Teacher of the Year Honor Roll—the first Indian honored in the program since its inception in 1952. The recognition symbolizes the importance of education and the achievements of gifted teachers everywhere. He was nominated by the Alaska Commissioner of Education for "his superior ability to impart knowledge and to instill intellectual curiosity and a love of learning."

In that same year, he was appointed by the governor of Alaska to serve on the Commission on Cross-Cultural Education, and was named as one of the members of the State of Alaska Textbook Commission.

Other high honors were to follow. An honorary Doctor's degree was conferred upon him by the University of Alaska, and he also received the Award of Merit for Distinguished Service, the highest award of the U.S. Department of the Interior.

He was honored by his alma mater when he attended the graduation exercises for his oldest daughter. Immediately after the ceremony, without pause, Mr. Demmert jetted back to Alaska so that he would be in time for the opening of his sixth-grade class in Sitka.

Archie Demmert has brought great honor to his state, as well as to himself, through his dedication to his profession and his contributions to young people. Always, his students have come first, and he has given to them those qualities which money can't buy, but which are vital to the future of our country.

James Gladstone

Statesman, rancher, politician, man of action—this was James Gladstone, the first Indian ever to be appointed to the Canadian Senate. He was born in Alberta on May 21, 1887, and was a Blood Indian, who, with the Piegans and the Blackfeet Indians of the United States, made up the Blackfeet Confederacy. This Indian nation was strong and powerful and one of the most colorful of the western Plains people.

When he was seven years old, James was placed in a mission school. He had a faculty for getting into trouble and was usually the butt of the older boys, who liked to make trouble for him when he didn't make it for himself.

A favorite trick was to throw him into the Indian graveyard near the school. Here the Indians placed their dead, wrapped in blankets, in the trees. At first the little boy was terribly frightened, but when he discovered that nothing happened to him, and that the dead were "very dead, indeed," he began to poke around among the burial bundles. He picked up two skulls and smuggled them into his dormitory, fastening them above the beds of the bullies who continually harassed him. At night these two boys would make

75

cigarettes and pass them around from bed to bed. When one boy struck a match to light his cigarette and saw the skulls grinning eerily down at him, he screamed in fright. The other boy fainted.

When the supervisor came to see what the trouble was, James buried his head in the blankets and pretended to be asleep. The skulls were removed and no one ever knew who had put them there, except the two bullies. They became James' fast friends after that.

It was at the mission school that James learned to speak English. Those who learned quickly and who spoke the best were given a few cents each Saturday. James was punished a number of times for continuing to speak in Blackfeet, but soon he was collecting his coins with the other English-speaking youngsters.

There were no toys or play equipment at the school, so James and the boys played Indian games. In the winter, they used beef ribs for skates. They threw mud balls at each other, and played bow and arrow games, and they didn't miss any "white man toys," for they had never had them.

While he was at school, James worked part-time on the mission farm. He learned to cut and plant potatoes, build root houses, and a number of other things which were to prove useful in later years. He stayed at the school until he was twelve and had completed the equivalent of eighth grade. Then he went to live with one of the mission teachers. He would interpret for this teacher and help him distribute food and clothing on his visits to the Indian families. At that time, the Bloods were living in log cabins in the winter, and in their tipis in the summer.

James would also look after the teacher's children and

HENRY
(HANK) ADAMS

LOUIS W. BALLARD

GEORGE BLUE SPRUCE

ROBERT L. BENNETT

LOUIS R. BRUCE

JARRETT BLYTHE

LEON COOK

Alan Rinzler

VINE DELORIA, JR.

JAMES GLADSTONE

ARCHIE DEMMERT

LaDONNA HARRIS

NED HATATHLI

ALLAN HOUSER

HAROLD S. JONES

WILLIAM W. KEELER

Navajo Tribe

PETER MacDONALD

BILLY MILLS

Bureau of Indian Affairs

N. SCOTT
MOMADAY

MARIA AND JULIAN MARTINEZ

HELEN L. PETERSON

BARNEY OLD COYOTE

BEN REIFEL

ARTHUR RAYMOND

EVERETT B.
RHOADES

ANNIE DODGE WAUNEKA

JOSEPH C. VASQUEZ

he went to the school run for the employees of the government's Indian Department.

One day, when out riding, he came upon the Bloods holding their sacred Sun Dance. This was a very important ritual and those who had not been brought up in the religion were not welcomed to it. James was attacked by a group of Indian police who guarded the Sun Dance camp. They chased him for about two miles before he eluded them. He was afraid to go back to the dance grounds, although he very much wanted to see what took place.

When the teacher with whom he lived moved away, James was taken to a day school by another teacher. He lived in the building, which was both house and school, and again he looked after the teacher's children. He also served the noon meal to the school children, carrying an iron kettle of beef broth and a barrel of hardtack into the classroom. He would set the kettle of broth on the pot-bellied stove and each child was given a cupful.

Later, James was sent to an industrial school, opened to teach trades to Anglican Indian students. He wanted to learn carpentry, but there was no instructor for this. So, he was put to work in the laundry and at washing dishes. This work he hated, and he asked if he could learn printing instead. He was an apt pupil, learning quickly how to set type, make up pages, and operate the foot press. He spent most of his time in the printing shop without attending any other classes.

James contracted a serious case of typhoid while at the industrial school. While he was convalescing, one of the employees claimed that some of her belongings had been stolen. In order to make the guilty one confess, the principal put all the boys on bread and water, even James, who was supposed to have a convalescent diet.

The hungry boys went on strike and refused to attend classes. They walked to Calgary where they begged for food and only returned to the school to sleep. Then they decided to run away. They walked all night, covering about twenty-six miles, following the railway tracks. They found a camp of Cree Indians and were taken in by them. James, barely recovered from his illness, became delirious and was unconscious when the Mounted Police finally caught up with the runaways.

The boys were returned to school and, to their surprise, were not punished for running away. But the dish of roast beans and pork, which was a well-liked meal on Wednesdays and Sundays, was cut in half. A short time later, the employee found her belongings.

James left the industrial school when he was eighteen. He worked as a printer, and then on various ranches, learning all that he could of ranching techniques. For a time he served as interpreter at the reserve mission, and then he was appointed scout and interpreter for the Royal Northwest Mounted Police.

During the first World War, Gladstone was employed on the Greater Production Effort to put large areas into crops to help the wartime program. In this work, he made an outstanding record.

Then he was appointed assistant stockman, and finally stockman, on the reservation, his work being to teach his fellow tribesmen the proper care of their cattle. The Blood reservation is the largest in Canada. Since they were given the reserve lands, they never surrendered any of it, although they were often under great pressure to do so. James recalled one incident when the head chief was approached about giving up part of the land.

"He bent down and picked a handful of grass," he remembered. " 'This you can use,' " he said. "Then he picked a handful of earth and pressed it to his heart and said: 'This is mine and will always be mine for my children of the future.' "

The Bloods never forgot these words, and so they hung onto their lands in spite of considerable hardship. When cattle were introduced on the reservation, many of the Indians did very well in looking after their herds. But the government induced them to handle the cattle as a single herd. As the years went by, the Indians only knew they had cattle when they received a check for sales from the Indian Agency office.

When severe losses were caused by bad winters, the herds dwindled to such an extent that the Indians were told to look after them again as individual herds. Some were glad to get their cattle back and became successful ranchers, but others had lost interest during the years that the herds were taken away from them. They sold them to other Indians or let them wander out of range.

James always pointed to this as an example of why Indians lost their initiative and confidence. "When they first settled on the reserve," he said, "most were anxious to work, but they lost this desire as more and more of their responsibilities were taken away from them. Attempts to restore their willingness to work made little headway. When a man is treated as a child for many years, he will be slow to take on responsibility."

Pointing out a number of incidents where he, himself, was hampered in assuming responsibility, James always counseled: "The great need is to assist and encourage Indian people to work their lands for themselves so they can support their families by their own efforts. On reserves such as mine, where there is good farming, the young men should be screened before being located. There are some people who would never make a success of farming, but might be happier raising cattle, or doing other work. They should be encouraged to do these things themselves without being under the direction of the agent."

Discouraged by the restrictive paternalism, James Gladstone quit farming altogether and went to work in the coal mines to support his wife and family. He didn't return to farming for three years. It was then that the Inspector of Indian Agencies asked him to return to his farm, as an example to other Indians who were giving up. He agreed but only on the condition that he would farm for himself and not under the direction of the Indian office.

Back on his own ranch, James began to build it up so that it became one of the finest on the reserve. He ran about 500 head of cattle and cultivated some 800 acres of land. He was the first to use power machinery, chemical sprays, and other modern methods and equipment. His house was the first on the reserve to have electricity.

Although he had been brought up in a mission school and was known as a progressive, James was also a supporter of native traditions and religious practices and was taken into membership in the ancient Crazy Dog Society, a secret fraternity.

Active as he was in the development of his own area, he was also devoted to the total Indian cause. He began to work in the interest of other tribes and he traveled extensively to meet with the tribal leaders in the western provinces.

He became president of the Indian Association of Alberta, serving two terms, and later was named honorary president of this body. He took a prominent role in drives for better education for Indians, greater respect for Indian treaty rights, and the participation of Indians in their own administration. On a number of occasions, he was a delegate to Ottawa to discuss proposed changes in the Indian Act.

All of this made an impact, and the quiet-spoken but firm man was highly respected in the Canadian seat of government.

In 1958, when he was seventy-one, he was appointed to the Senate. He was named co-chairman of the joint Senate-Commons Committee on Indian Affairs and through the recommendations of this Committee, reservation Indians became eligible to vote in federal elections. Until that took place, Senator Gladstone had never been able to vote in a Canadian election.

In his maiden speech to the Senate, Senator Gladstone spoke a few words in his native tongue. He said: "The Indians of Canada are very happy to know they have someone in Ottawa to represent them in the government of Canada. I pray that I will be able to speak the right words for them." He also said, "I have always tried to do the best I could for the Indians and now I will have greater opportunities. I'll talk only when I have something important or significant to say."

He concluded with these words: "I hope that you will all be patient with me in the months ahead, for this is a new tribe for me. I have much to learn, not only about the workings of our government, but of the problems and needs of my people all across Canada. When I speak for the Indians, it will be only for them, and not for those who are trying to tell them what to do. I want to be their voice in Ottawa until they all choose to take the federal vote for themselves."

Senator Gladstone had many significant things to say while he was in the Senate. He reaffirmed his belief in education for Indians many times, saying: "If we are to become a success in anything today, we must be properly educated, not only in academic subjects but in learning the life way of the white man. If our people are to compete in business and industry with the white man, we must be given the kind of education that will be good enough and broad enough for this purpose. If they are to live on reserves where they must earn their living in other ways, they should be given the kind of education that will be of practical use to them."

In his young manhood, he pointed out, "I received practically no help or encouragement in sending my two daughters away to train as nurses and another as stenographer. They were the first from my reserve, out of a population of more than 2,000, to enter these fields. This was more than sixty years after the Bloods had settled on their reservation."

In the Senator's opinion, Indian children who left the reservations for schooling, or who went to nongovernment schools, would grow up without feelings of inferiority. Indians from the government schools, where they mingled only with Indians, felt a barrier on leaving the reservation and did not mix well with white people, he said. He advocated that the government schools be turned into trade schools, particularly for pupils in the sixteen- to nineteen-year age bracket.

While he favored integration, he was against any suggestion to abolish the Indian reserves. Integration had to be voluntary, he said. He wanted to make the reserves self-sufficient economically, mostly by giving more authority to Indian agents who could act as reserve managers.

Senator Gladstone retired from the Senate in 1971 because

of failing health. He expressed the hope that he would see
one Indian representative from each province in the Senate
in the future. He placed much faith in the young Indian
leaders who were coming to the fore, and who were making
themselves heard. They were actively engaged in getting
things done for their people, he said, and he admired their
new initiative, new thinking, and new aggressiveness.

When the Canadian government presented its so-called
"White Paper," which was a plan for action pertaining to
Indians, there was a hue and cry of protest from Indians
all over Canada. Senator Gladstone believed that the White
Paper, and the reaction to its proposals, was instrumental in
uniting the Indian people. "They got together to hammer out
their response to it. I was amazed at how they argued and
threshed out each point publicly before the Minister. I was
proud of them. The young Indians showed they could hold
their own and take part effectively in Canadian affairs."

The Red Paper, which the Indians presented in rebuttal,
he felt "embraced the thinking of the Indian peoples. It was
done in a business-like manner. It was a document properly
prepared, carefully thought out, and both well presented
and well received."

Senator Gladstone died suddenly of a heart attack shortly
after his retirement. He was eighty-four years old. He had
lived through an age of apathy and suppression, but he lived
to see the dawning of a new age in Indian politics under new,
young leadership and, to him, this was a great source of
satisfaction. He had played no small part in bringing it about.

LaDonna Harris

W<small>HEN</small> LaDonna Harris makes a speech—as she frequently does—and says, "I am a Comanche," she stands a little taller, a little straighter, and her eyes flash with pride. There is a reason for this.

When she was a girl growing up in Oklahoma, it wasn't "socially acceptable" to be an Indian. She often heard slighting remarks, or was made to feel inferior by non-Indian neighbors, and this hurt.

Worse than that, her white father left her Indian mother because of the hostility expressed in subtle and not so subtle ways. He went to live in California, and though he kept in touch with his family by letter, he never returned.

"I used to dream that some day I would grow up and be important and do something wonderful that would make him want to see me," LaDonna says. The dreams were poignant, but she didn't waste too much time in indulging them. Rather, she set about to make them come true.

LaDonna was raised by her grandparents and in their home only Comanche was spoken. The grandfather, the Eagle Medicine Man of the tribe, had been a member of the famous scouts, Indian Troop L at Fort Sill. A proud Co-

manche, he wore braids all his life. But he enjoyed watching
television and for this he always put on his best suit of
clothes. He figured that if he could see the people on the
TV screen, they must be able to see him also. One of the
programs that he liked to watch was "Ding Dong School."
When Miss Frances, the program teacher, said, "How are you
today?" he always answered her politely.

In high school, LaDonna met her husband, Fred, who was
to become United States Senator from Oklahoma. He was the
son of a poor sharecropper and the early years of marriage
were a constant struggle. Fred worked his way through college on scholarships and LaDonna worked, also, to help put
him through school with degrees in political science and law.

It was then that LaDonna became interested in education,
especially education for Indians. She served this cause in
many ways, and in 1969 was awarded the National Education Association's Human Rights Award. She is a member of
the Board of Visitors of the University of Oklahoma and a
member of the Board of Trustees of Antioch College.

With her feelings of compassion for the underdog, stemming directly from her girlhood experiences, she was natu-
rally drawn to the fields of minority rights and poverty. Another interest was the improvement of health and mental
health care, and her husband shared in these interests. She
has been a member of many committees and boards in all of
these areas, and in 1967 was appointed Chairman of the
Women's National Advisory Council on Poverty. She was a
member of the National Committee Against Discrimination
in Housing, of the National Rural Housing Conference, and
a chairman of the Health Task Force of the National Steering Committee of the Urban Coalition. She was on the board
of the National Association of Mental Health and was chair-

man of the 1970 National Health Forum. She is on the board
of the National Health Council.

She went back and forth across the state of Oklahoma,
visiting hospitals and facilities for the care of the impover-
ished or the mentally ill. She made many public appearances,
and when her husband decided to enter politics, she did all
she could to further this career which led to his becoming
a Senator from Oklahoma. She also worked the "campaign
circuit" when he came up for re-election at the end of his
term.

In spite of her many activities, she never neglected her
three children, all of whom have Comanche names and who
are extremely proud of their Indian blood.

When the Harris family went to Washington, it was expected that there would be Indian activity. LaDonna had
the reputation, by then, of being tough, smart, and angry;
these three qualities would make her a dedicated exponent
of the Indian cause. Her husband often referred to her
humorously, but admiringly, as a "fierce and warlike Comanche."

"The national Indian policy," LaDonna said, "has been
one of pulling the Indian away from the community—all-
Indian schools, all-Indian hospitals, all-Indian organizations.
This does not help Indians to become contributing members
of society; it strengthens prejudice through lack of understanding."

Non-Indians think Indians are dumb, lazy, dishonest, al-
coholic, unable to learn, she points out, and Indians withdraw and expect only unfriendliness and rebuffs and fear to
try to compete with others.

"Both attitudes must change if substantial progress is to

come," Mrs. Harris says, as she continues to crusade for Indians.

One of her first acts was to found Oklahomans for Indian Opportunity, a private organization committed to helping Indians help themselves and develop their talents and resources. Supported by a grant under the federal antipoverty program, OIO set out at once to attack "gut problems." Students were given counseling in everything from educational and career possibilities to social adjustment. Remedial instruction was given where needed, and older people were pushed into community activities. Families leaving rural areas and going to the cities for employment were given assistance until they had become independent.

LaDonna was president of the new organization and from her fertile brain came many ideas that immediately found implementation and brought Indians forward in their home state in ways that had never before happened.

When the Harris family visited South and Central America, LaDonna became greatly interested in the Peace Corps. Visiting every Indian community that they could, they found that few of the people knew what the Peace Corps was or, if they did know, they suspected its motivations.

LaDonna came home with the idea that Indians from this country should be trained to work with Latin American Indians, since they would be *simpático* and there would be an understanding that would not be possible among other Peace Corps workers.

With LaDonna, to have an idea is to put it into action. So, through her Oklahoma association, the Peace Pipe Project was born. The Project was open to Indians throughout the country, who would be assigned to service in Latin America after a number of weeks of special training. The Peace Pipe

Project was administered in cooperation with the Peace Corps.

LaDonna's crusading soon attracted attention among the Washington administrative personnel and she was named by President Lyndon Johnson to serve on the newly-formed National Commission on Indian Opportunity. This group was the responsibility of the Vice President.

When the administration changed, LaDonna resigned and prepared to do battle. The interest was sincere, she said, "but the Commission got bogged down in red tape and feet dragging, and nothing was being accomplished because no one was pushing." She then founded her own means of "push." This was Americans for Indian Opportunity, similar to the Oklahoma organization but much broader in scope.

"Indians have been the victims of fine rhetoric, followed by inaction or worse, for two centuries," LaDonna said. "Swift action is what is needed."

Washington headquarters were opened with the support of many public figures and prominent Indian leaders. It isn't unusual to find LaDonna plugging away long after most offices have closed—even to licking the stamps for the day's mail.

Work for Indians has to be done at both federal and state levels, Mrs. Harris says. The Bureau of Indian Affairs is the favorite whipping boy, but "in discussing Indian problems you have to make it society's attitude as a whole and not just that of the BIA."

In outlining the program for Americans for Indian Opportunity, she listed a two-way educational program, with the government learning more about Indians, their desires and feelings, and the Indians learning more about how to live with the government and how to obtain governmental benefits and opportunities perhaps unknown to them. Also, work with and through local Indian groups, helping them organize and secure funds for their own projects, was another point.

Included were the formation of youth councils, job development and on-the-job training, college recruiting and scholarship programs. The group will also serve as a national clearinghouse for Indian and non-Indian volunteers to work with Indian tribes and organizations.

Another goal would be an intern program through which young whites would be placed in Indian homes and reservations, with Indian youngsters to be placed in city homes in a sort of cultural exchange.

"I'm not on the warpath," Mrs. Harris says. "It is phrases like that which reinforce the stereotypes that whites have about Indians. White ideas about Indians are completely phony and I am seeking ways to correct them. We don't sit around doing beadwork and making baskets all the time. We are out being active, good Americans and making our way in American life.

"It is one of my hopes to change the idea that the Indian is a problem," Mrs. Harris comments. "Many of the history books are the reason why so many people have misconceptions about Indians. They also tend to generalize about Indians and this can't be done. There are many different tribes of Indians—some two hundred of them—each with its own very distinct culture.

"In my state of Oklahoma, there are more than 100 different tribes and 69 different languages spoken. There are more Indians in Oklahoma than in any other state, and Indians, especially the Five Civilized Tribes, played prominent roles in the state's history.

"Yet, few Oklahomans know that the Cherokees built the first school in Oklahoma and that they established the first formal education west of the Mississippi River. Instead of bringing out such facts, the history books stress the 'savage, ignorant Indian, the poor Indian that can't learn, the lazy Indian.'

"The history books have had a major part in building the stereotyped Indian, and these labels push them apart from society because society doesn't know and doesn't understand."

Indians get confused and frustrated by these stereotypes, too, Mrs. Harris states. "They don't know who they are or where they fit into society because they have been pushed here and there and because of the mental images concerning them."

Teachers need to help Indian young people build good self-images, LaDonna emphasizes. "If the Indian is thought of as being lazy, he will think of himself as he is thought of in his community. This kind of stereotyping is one of the most vicious forms of discrimination."

Looking down on people is no way to approach them, LaDonna Harris says. "Attitudes that are preachy or pitying are very harmful. Indians don't want to feel that they are being helped because they are poor and ignorant, or because others are better than they and they must be raised up from a lower level. Such attitudes evoke anger and hostility in Indians which can lead to outright trouble."

According to Mrs. Harris, the high rate of Indian school drop-outs comes at the age when they become aware of socialization. The difference society puts on skin color, clothes, and money is important to the impressional teen-

ager, for it is at this age they are aware of boy-girl relationships.

"Indians are highly sensitive people to begin with, and
if made to feel even more sensitive, they withdraw into a
shell and make no further effort to break down barriers."

Ned Hatathli

In a small hogan in a canyon on the Navajo Reservation, a boy child was born. It was a crisp autumn day and the trees were turning gold. That night the great fall Yeibechai ceremony would be held, when the gods would be asked for special favors.

The baby was the first child in a family that was to number ten children. His parents were traditionalists, and the child —Ned Hatathli—would be brought up in the traditional way. When he was barely out of babyhood, he was taught to care for the few sheep and horses owned by his parents, their only means of livelihood. He herded the animals to pasture and to water and watched over them so that no maurauding wolf would approach or they would stray too far away.

Ned's uncle was a policeman at the agency town where the government buildings and staff were located. He was a firm believer in schooling and often rounded up those children whose parents kept them out of school, and delivered them to the school officials.

As Ned grew older, his uncle talked constantly to his parents about sending him to school. When he was six, his family finally agreed and the boy went with his uncle. He was taken to the government boarding school at Tuba City where everything was strange and bewildering. He had never been in a white man's house before. His clothing was strange, the language was strange, and while his teachers were kind, they, too, were strange, with white faces instead of Indian copper-colored ones.

But Ned was an eager boy, filled with curiosity, and it wasn't long before he settled down and adjusted to the new situation. He wasn't much impressed with school, however, and took things as a matter of course until he became twelve years old.

In that year, a group of students was taken on a summer tour of the Deep South. For the first time, he entered the world outside of the reservation. He saw great crowds of people, and among them black faces, which startled and intrigued him. The large industrial cities were amazing with their belching smokestacks, tall buildings, and fine houses.

There were wonderful farms which were in great contrast to the Navajo fields with their few crops of corn, beans, and melons, and which the Indians somehow managed to cultivate in spite of little water.

And most wonderful of all was the ocean! If only there could be an ocean back home, he thought. Any Navajo would give a lot to have water like that. Almost, he didn't believe the ocean.

All of the things he saw aroused him to the degree that he decided that education was important after all—perhaps the most important thing he had to do.

For a time, Ned was kept out of school because of illness. Numerous ceremonies called "sings" were held to cure him, because his people knew nothing of doctors or hospitals.

They lived in a remote part of the reservation and they were entirely Indian in their way of life.

The time at home was beneficial for Ned, however. In the evening, there were long hours of storytelling when he learned of Navajo beliefs and heroes. He closely identified with the customs and traditions of his people and his whole life was enriched by the experience.

When he was well again, Ned was once more eager to return to school and pursue his education. He rode the thirty miles back to the boarding school on horseback, because he had no other way to get there, and never again did he live in the family hogan, the log and earth home of the Navajos.

When he completed high school, Ned had been such a good student that he was valedictorian of his class. He then went to Lawrence, Kansas, to Haskell Institute, one of the largest government schools for Indians to which students came from all over the country. He had never seen so many different kinds of Indians, nor did he dream they existed.

Ned stayed only six months at Haskell, for World War II broke out and he volunteered for service in the Navy. He was nineteen years old. The Navy meant the ocean and he wanted to travel on that water and see what it was really like. The ocean drew him like a magnet.

In the Navy, he studied radio communication and was radio operator aboard a tanker in the South Pacific. He visited Australia, New Guinea, the Philippines, and many other ports in that area, and he learned that the ocean was even larger than he had thought it to be.

With military duty behind him at the war's end, he re-entered Haskell to complete a post-high school commercial course. He then returned to the reservation where he worked for the government Indian Service as a property clerk and where he met and married a Navajo girl.

A year later, the young couple's first child, a girl, was born. Ned then decided to return to school. At Haskell, he had been labelled with a "not college potential" tag, but this he chose to ignore. He had set goals for himself, and he needed more schooling to achieve them.

Accepted at Arizona State College (now Northern Arizona University), Ned buckled down to work. He had little money, and so he helped to finance his schooling by making and selling moccasins. He also made and sold paintings and gained a good reputation in both fields.

In his first year in college, Ned was elected to membership in the national honorary society for freshmen, Kappa Delta Pi. Before he graduated, he was named also to Phi Eta Sigma, given the Blue Key, selected for Kappa Phi Kappa, and he was to have the national honorary Phi Kappa Phi awarded to him. His bachelor's degree carried with it distinction in art and education.

Back on the reservation, the Navajo people were beginning to stir themselves in various ways. Navajo weaving was then at its lowest level and this had been one of the tribe's great distinctions. Navajo rugs, when well made, are among the finest in the world.

The tribe had formed an arts and crafts guild and Ned was asked to become its first Indian manager. He built this guild into one of the tribe's most important resources. He brought new life to the weaving industry, insisting upon top quality work and the restoration of the old traditional designs.

A master of design, he modernized the traditional Navajo silver work so that it would have higher sales value. Some pieces were too "barbaric" or too heavy for modern tastes, so he developed a combination of old and new that won approval and established this craft on a new level. Modern designs were encouraged, provided that something of the old remained. Not only did Ned revitalize the entire craft industry, but he developed a sound base and formula for profitable marketing.

In a short time, Ned Hatathli was elected to the Tribal Council and to its Advisory Council. He was also made chairman of the Resources Committee and charter board member of the Navajo Forest Products Industry, a new industry which was putting down infant roots.

And now he was to begin a period of tremendous service. Resigning from the Tribal Council, he was made Director of Tribal Resources, the first to hold this position. He proceeded to put into motion the most extensive and intensive natural resources development that the tribe had ever known. Oil and gas production burgeoned. A huge coal-fired power plant was built which partly provided electricity for a vast area, and coal mining was stepped up. Uranium was mined and processed in two newly constructed plants.

All over the reservation, there was the hum of activity. A tribal timber management plant was erected and also a modern "dream" sawmill that is outstanding in its completeness and efficiency. There were man-made lakes where only small ponds had existed and there were plans for dam construction.

Livestock programs evolved and were implemented, and livestock associations formed. A tremendous irrigation project was initiated and negotiations for reservation-based industrial plants to train and employ Navajos were begun.

It was an incredible period of growth and promise, and Ned Hatathli was a prime mover in all of it.

After seven years, Ned became Education Specialist with the Navajo Irrigation Project, now well on its way. As such, he developed agri-education programs with schools and functioned in a public relations capacity.

But all of this time, another Navajo dream had been taking shape. It was the feeling among most of the tribal leaders that Indians should have a stake in Indian education, and that this education should include that which was directly related to Navajo needs and concerns.

Taking a giant step forward, the tribe founded the Navajo Community College and Ned Hatathli was chosen as the Executive Vice President. Classes began in 1969—the first institution of higher education ever established by Indians on an Indian reservation. In that same year, he became the first Indian president of the college and he started a new era in the development of human resources.

The college is much much more than a great accomplishment—it is a symbol of the "impossible dream" for which men reached and made come true. "It stands," Mr. Hatathli says, "for Indians controlling their own destiny."

Once, when asked what made the college different, he replied with just a shade of rarely permitted irritation: "Well, we don't teach that Columbus discovered America!"

Navajo Community College is pride in being an Indian—a Navajo; it is pride in Indian culture; it is a love of Indian ways and of Indian country, Mr. Hatathli says. Even the architecture reflects this pride, for some of the buildings are shaped like the hogan, the traditional eight-sided house of the Navajos.

The college is almost completely innovative. In its adult

education program, some of the older Navajos are learning to write their own names for the first time. For many of them, too, it is the first time they have seen written Navajo, and this helps them to understand English more quickly. And they are helped to see the meaning and value of education in the lives of their children.

Talented Navajo silversmiths teach this ancient craft, although they may be without formal education. The idea is to utilize Navajo talents regardless of the individual's background. Sales of choice pieces help to give the school revenue.

Navajo women teach the fine art of rug weaving and, again, this is of economic value.

Other courses taught at the school include Navajo history and culture, the Navajo language, creative writing on Navajo subjects, Indians of the Americas, Indian law and government, and exploring Indian art. But there is also a full complement of courses in academic subjects, from English and mathematics to business and agriculture.

"What we are trying to do," President Hatathli says, "is to take the best from the white man's culture and the best from Indian culture. We believe we can learn from the white man, but we believe that we can teach the white man, too."

Ned Hatathli, the "not college potential," was given the Distinguished Citizen Award from his Alma Mater as well as an honorary doctor of laws degree from Eastern Michigan University. He has been awarded the Silver Beaver Award by the Boy Scouts for his contributions to Scouting, and the Indian Achievement Award for his accomplishments as an individual and for his contributions for the benefit of his people, which are far-reaching in effect.

Perhaps the most meaningful of all of the recognition that

has come to him was the passage at the end of 1971 by the House and Senate, and the signing by President Richard Nixon, of a bill providing federal funding for construction and operational support of the unique school which he heads.

Allan Houser

At one time, the Apaches were the most feared and hated tribe in the Southwest. They were fierce fighters and skilled raiders and they refused to give up their wild, free life to settle on a reservation.

The most noted of their war leaders was the wily Geronimo. Once the tribe had finally capitulated and accepted reservation life, Geronimo several times led his followers away and escaped with them into Mexico. From a hidden stronghold, he laid waste the Arizona settlements and the very mention of his name caused people to panic.

Geronimo was finally captured and was sent, with others, to prison in Florida. Eventually, he was returned to Oklahoma to live on the reservation at Fort Sill. Geronimo then became a man of peace. He was a successful farmer, and on "dress-up" occasions he wore a stovepipe hat. He even allowed himself to be photographed at the steering wheel of an automobile and to be exhibited at the St. Louis World's Fair. He also rode in President Theodore Roosevelt's inaugural parade.

Allan Houser is the great-grandson of the famous Geronimo. He was born on the reservation in 1914, and he helped his father with the small farm, going to school only intermittently. His childhood was one of great hardship, but this did not prevent him from carving out an outstanding art career, for he is one of the foremost Indian artists and sculptors, and a credit to the field of art at large.

In school, Allan directed his energies toward professional athletics, but a serious illness diverted him from this. To pass the time while he was confined, he turned to drawing and discovered that here was something in which he excelled.

Like most of his boyhood companions, he had been brought up on stories of the "good old days," when the Apaches were in their glory and when the Indians rode to hunt the buffalo, pitting their strength and their bows against the huge animal.

So indelibly were those stories impressed on Allan's mind that some of his first paintings were of the buffalo hunt. His work was the epitome of tensed action, with the feeling of motion and vitality caught in a few simple lines.

Before he graduated from high school, Allan had received his school's trophy for his outstanding art. His work was strong with human appeal, subtle in the use of color, and with splendid action. He would cleverly catch the full details of an Apache face, and the full details of costume. While he painted in the typical Indian two-dimensional style, his outlines were clean and definitive. He could say a very great deal with only a few marks of the brush, depicting a scene of great sadness or of great humor with equal impact.

When Allan left school, he opened his own studio in Santa Fe and held a number of one-man shows throughout the country. He began making a name for himself and was invited to paint some of the Indian murals in the Department of the Interior building in Washington.

His paintings were exhibited at the New York and San Francisco World's Fairs, and in Geneva, Switzerland. At one time he was asked to demonstrate his work to art students in China.

For a time, Allan was art instructor at Haskell Indian School. While there, he completed his first marble statue, "Comrades in Mourning," dedicated as a memorial to Haskell students who lost their lives in World War II.

The statue, a brooding figure, was then the first one completed by an Indian artist. It amply illustrated that the maker had great talent, not only with paint but with the chisel as well.

While at Haskell, Allan received a Guggenheim Fellowship in painting and sculpturing. This was a signal honor and his studies under the Fellowship added a strength and depth of maturity to his work without sacrificing any of the "Houser significance." His works are quite recognizable, for no one has been able to capture his distinctive style.

For a time, Allan taught at Intermountain Indian School in Utah and he also illustrated a number of books for adults and children. Then he became a member of the faculty of the Institute of American Indian Arts in Santa Fe and still teaches there, specializing in both painting and sculpture. His students have turned out some outstanding pieces in both media.

While at Intermountain, Allan was commissioned to create a mural and four dioramas for the Southern Plains Indian Museum and Crafts Center in Oklahoma. These are important features of the museum's permanent public displays.

Participating in many major art shows and exhibitions, Allan captured numerous awards, among them five grand awards. He was among the first to assist the Philbrook Museum in Tulsa in establishing its annual Indian art show and was awarded the Waite Phillips Trophy by Philbrook for his outstanding contributions.

Allan stays primarily with scenes from Apache life and Apache figures, for here he is most at home. His painting which won a Grand Prize in the third Philbrook show expresses much of the stoicism which is markedly characteristic of this quiet man. He has little to say, for he does his talking through his art. But he is well liked by his students who consider it an honor to be in his classes. He isn't an unfriendly person, merely reticent, and he places his art before conversation. Rarely does he comment on Indians as artists or what they should be as artists, for this is a matter of individual ability and inclination, he feels.

The painting which won the Grand Prize award at the Philbrook show in 1948 is entitled "Burying the Baby." A simple ground line carries across the paper, dipping downward to form an open grave. Standing at the side are an Apache man and woman with a small child clinging to the woman's skirts. Near the grave is the baby cradle with a few items scattered on the ground, one a basket water bottle, still made by the Apaches. The face of the woman shows that emotions are held back. The father's lips are parted; probably he is singing a last song to the baby. The colors are soft and muted and the whole effect is one of great solemnity and sadness. It is one of Allan Houser's more famous paintings.

In late 1971, Allan held his first major all-sculpture show at the Southern Plains Indian Museum. Twelve sculptures in bronze, steel, stone, and wood were on display. Each piece was conceived with a highly-integrated, aesthetic, and technical approach which has become Allan's hallmark in this field. The pieces were a broad spectrum of subject matter, ranging from genre to depictions of animal and mythical themes. A four-page illustrated brochure was published in connection with the display.

Allan Houser has spent thirty years of his life in teaching Indian students and has seen many of his pupils go on to professional success. He has never been static in his heart, and he encourages his students to experiment and innovate. Although he also takes on new dimensions, he never loses his own dynamic form and method. His work, even in sculpture, remains unmistakably Indian, and unmistakably Allan Houser.

It is obvious that his art has welled from deep roots with little outside influence. Study and training have served to emphasize this quality rather than detract from it. His art is not so much beautiful as it is virile. There is here and there a touch of delicacy, as in the leaves of a yucca plant, but the over-all effect is one of living and breathing, of a highly personal outlook, and of a strong emotional base.

Even as he develops new forms in new media, Allan Houser will still give to his art the aura of tradition.

Harold S. Jones

HAROLD S. JONES was born in South Dakota in 1909. His mother died when he was a small child and he was reared by his grandparents who lived on the Santee Sioux Reservation. The grandfather was a well-known Indian Episcopal priest who worked with the Indians on the Santee and Standing Rock reservations.

Harold came to have a love for the church early in life. He idolized his grandfather and would go with him on some of his rounds to the homes of parishoners. He was deeply impressed by the way his grandfather comforted those in distress and by the way faces would light up when he climbed down from his buggy to minister to those who needed him.

The Sioux people were desperately poor and his grandfather had only a small income, but he was always willing to share what he had with someone else.

Then came the day when his grandfather died. Harold remembers it as the saddest day in his life, for he suffered a deep loss. Not only that, there was no money to support the family. Harold feared that he might not be able to follow his grandfather into the ministry as his heart was set on doing.

"I like to think that God called me to the church," Harold says. "This was the only vocation that I wanted to follow. I wanted to be as good a priest as my grandfather had been."

But his family—the grandmother and brothers and sisters— had to be supported, so Harold threw back his shoulders and found work with a railroad crew. A sensitive young man, he did not enjoy the rough labor, or the company of the rougher men. But out of his pay he was able to send some money home and this made up for the rest of it.

When he was finally able to enter college, he had to keep on working to finance himself. "It was really tough going," he remembers. Finally, he had to drop out altogether. There was no way for an Indian to get educational assistance at that time and there was no one who could help him.

To sustain himself, he worked at anything that came his way. At one time he played semiprofessional baseball. Then, the government inaugurated a scholarship program for Indians. With help from this source and with what he had been able to put away, he went back to college to complete his studies.

Then came the matter of seminary training. Help came from the church and he entered Seabury Seminary in Evanston, Illinois. But the help was small for his needs, and Harold still had to make one nickel do the work of two.

"I used to go to meetings that were held by an Indian organization in Chicago," he says. "I always enjoyed attending, for the people were friendly and the programs interesting. Also, I met other Indians there who were making a go of it in the city. Finally, I guess the people grew tired of seeing me come so often without joining. They gently reminded me that the membership fee was only $1.00.

"I couldn't tell them that $1.00 looked like $5.00 to me. I just couldn't spare it. It took a whole twenty-five cents just to get into the city from Evanston and another to return. I couldn't spare a dollar on top of that."

He wanted to explain, but he couldn't. Pride wouldn't let him, so he pleaded studies and didn't go so often. Apparently the people understood, however, for they did what they could to help him. He had a fine singing voice and they were able to place him on club programs now and again as a speaker and singer, and for a fee.

Life in Evanston was vastly different from life on the reservation. In a college town, there are many activities and Harold took advantage of every one that was free, or that was arranged for seminary students. There were fine churches in the town and in Chicago, and he heard many of the great church leaders speak, or conduct services.

A cousin lived in Chicago and she and a coterie of girl friends would take Harold out to a Chinese restaurant for dinner, or to a roller skating rink, or for walks along the lake. Life was very pleasant and he was sorry when his theological training came to an end, although he was eager to begin his religious duties.

"My personal struggle seemed to have placed me in a redemptive and receptive relationship before the Creator and his creative force. Through it my life became a Christian adventure and was made worthwhile," he says. "False feelings of inferiority, selfishness, and the like were overcome."

Harold began his life work as a missionary on the Pine Ridge Reservation back in Sioux country. He was ordained to the diaconate at the reservation church by the Bishop of

South Dakota who had also ordained him to the priesthood. He understood the people, for he was one of them, and they understood him.

Later, he was sent among the Sioux Indians on the Cheyenne River Reservation. On both reservations, the conditions were discouraging. There was little to relieve the bleakness of life, and it was a constant struggle to keep the church going. The young minister had to work long hours, and travel long distances, and live on a meagre salary, but there was never any thought of turning to something else. He still felt that his footsteps were directed by God and that he had been led to serve his Indian people, and he stayed among them for eighteen years.

Then he was stationed in Wahpeton, North Dakota, as priest of Trinity Church. "Because I have English blood as well as Indian, I like to work where races need each other," Harold says, "and the church was a mixed parish."

He was also appointed religious counselor to the students at Wahpeton Indian School.

"Some of these youngsters had very severe problems. Some came from broken homes, or had trouble in mastering their studies, or found it hard to be confined to classrooms when school was not to their liking. They needed a friend, someone they could talk to and who would know why they felt as they did—and I tried to be that friend," Harold says.

He would say to the youngsters, "As Indian people we must recognize that we have been created by God with a purpose and an equality as have been all people. God can make each one of the best. We must have confidence in ourselves and realize as a race that we have great contributions to make to our wonderful country. This faith and all that you learn at school must be looked upon as the necessary means for becoming creative forces in life."

This he believes with great sincerity.

In 1968, Harold was sent as vicar to the Good Shepherd Mission on the Navajo Reservation. He organized and directed a leadership training program which was designed to get Indian people "involved in doing."

"Unless we learn to do things for ourselves, we're not going to be involved or operate at full capacity," he told those taking part. He was not certain how well he would be received by the Navajos, an aloof and often inscrutable people. He could not speak a word of Navajo, and here were a people of entirely different culture and customs.

Again he felt that God had directed his footsteps, and he found that he was accepted and that he was making progress. Although he could speak his own language fluently, Navajo was much more difficult, but he learned how to sing hymns in the language, or, if he could not manage the syllables, at least he followed the tune, and he could guide others in reading the scriptures in Navajo.

The training program was operating successfully when Harold was asked to return to South Dakota, this time as Suffragen Bishop for the state, working with both Indian and non-Indian groups.

He is the first Indian ever elected a bishop in the history of the Episcopal Church, and his election came 102 years after another Santee Sioux Indian, Paul Mazakute, was ordained to the ministry.

Bishop Jones is a quiet, rather than dynamic, leader, but he is a leader nevertheless, with a record of fine accomplishment. Although there were times when it would have been easier to give up than to keep trying, he never swerved from the goal he had set for himself, and this firmness of purpose he imparts to others. To him, it is evident that God is truly a creative force and his life has been an expression of that deep conviction.

"To know definitely the future of a race is not granted to any of us," Bishop Jones says. "However, it is possible to determine a likely direction from a study of the past and the present.

"One of our outstanding chiefs once said: 'Had it not been for the arrival of Christianity, we of the Plains people might have been exterminated.' Better than a hundred years later, we find ourselves the Indian Americans of our time. We memorialize our fathers and the missionaries of yesterday who helped them by not merely saying Amen to close an experience, or even history itself. Rather, we say a loud and meaningful Amen by rolling up our sleeves in an effort to use our new vision, new courage, and new strength."

William W. Keeler

A<small>MONG</small> the Cherokee people, there has been no greater leader than John Ross, who fought against the removal of the tribe from their eastern homelands, and then led them over the "Trail of Tears" to Indian Territory. There, he helped them to re-establish themselves, to set up their government, to found schools, and to continue to progress from the already high level of advancement which was theirs at the time of the removal.

William Wayne Keeler is often called "the greatest leader since Ross" by modern-day Cherokee people. He was appointed Principal Chief of the Cherokees by President Harry Truman in 1949, and in 1971 he was elected to this office by an overwhelming majority under a new law giving the tribes the right to elect their leaders.

Bill Keeler has held so many important offices in business and civic circles, and has received so many honors from Indians and non-Indians alike, that this record would fill a complete volume by itself. President of Phillips Petroleum Company since 1967, he has been president also of the National Association of Manufacturers. He has been chosen by the American Academy of Achievement as one of fifty giants

111

of accomplishment from the great fields of endeavor to receive the "Golden Plate Award." He has received the Indian Achievement Award, and the Distinguished Service Citation, the highest honor of the University of Oklahoma. He has been elected to the Oklahoma Hall of Fame and he has been awarded several honorary degrees by various universities.

Keeler was born in Texas in 1908, but as a child was sent to live with his maternal grandmother in Oklahoma because of his mother's illness. The grandmother spoke only Cherokee. She was only one generation away from the "Trail of Tears," and although she had married a white man, she was still very suspicious of white people.

The grandmother wanted young Bill to grow up as an Indian boy. She saw to it that he spoke only Cherokee, and she imprinted constantly on his mind, through stories, the image of Indian courage and honesty, their greatness as a people, and the greatness of John Ross.

She also saw to it that the boy met others of his clan— the Long Hair Clan—because Cherokees of the same clan are considered to be brothers and sisters, even though not related by blood. The older people are considered mothers and fathers. Clan descent was counted through the mother's side, and Keeler's own father's clan was of no significance.

During his life with his grandmother, the home was constantly filled with Indians just "dropping in" and the table was always crowded with unexpected guests. There were always plenty of dogs around the place, too. Grandmother would adopt any stray that wandered by, and at one time, Bill had twelve dogs of his own. He also had horses, pet coons, squirrels, rabbits, and other animals, and he learned to imitate the calls of these and other wild creatures. He learned to hunt and track like any other Cherokee boy. "The excitement of discovering I had caught an animal and the serious problem that developed when it turned out to be a skunk is still vividly remembered," Mr. Keeler says.

When his mother recovered and he returned to live with her, the whole situation of upbringing was reversed. His mother had attended a Quaker school for Indians and she had experienced some unhappy slights because she was considered a "second-class citizen." She wanted Bill to forget his Indian background and grow up as a white boy. She never spoke Cherokee or permitted him to do so and the effect was one of almost denial of Indian blood. However, she held to the Cherokee principles of rigid integrity and honest dealing with others and these were preserved as qualities of character.

Indian people are characteristically retiring and introverted. Individuals do not rise one above the other. "Push" and aggression are not admired; modesty and humility and a concern for the group are inherent. As he grew older and went out into the world to earn his way, Bill Keeler found it difficult to overcome this Indian side of his nature. He missed out a number of times because he held back and could not sell himself or present his views when asked them.

When he was sixteen he began his oil industry experience by working during the summers in the oil fields for Phillips. He joined Phillips permanently while a student at the University of Kansas and held down a full-time refinery job while continuing his studies. He went steadily up the ladder as a chemist, process engineer, night superintendent and chief process engineer. He was promoted to technical assistant to the vice president of the refining department. Then he became vice president of that department, then of the executive department, and finally executive vice president.

During World War II he represented Phillips in Mexico as project manager for the construction of a new refinery. The United States government supplied the critical materials for this refinery and selected the Phillips Company as technical supervisor. Keeler also served during the war as chairman or member of various refining technical committees of the Petroleum Administration of War.

In 1952, he was again picked for defense service on a full-time basis (without compensation) as Director of Refining, Petroleum Administration for Defense. In 1960, he headed the first United States Petroleum Industry Exchange Delegation on a tour of the Russian oil industry.

When Mr. Keeler became Principal Chief of the Cherokees, he became very active in educational and welfare work among his people. "Indians should not be entitled to more rights than anybody else, but they should have all the rights that anyone else has." He set about seeing that the Cherokees would have lost rights restored to them, and to initiate projects that would bring improved economy to the Cherokee people.

He was instrumental in shaping legislation which resulted in the tribe's receiving an award of $14,789,000 from the government as readjustment of a land sale made by the Indians to the government many years ago.

He established the Cherokee Foundation to promote the welfare and culture of the tribe and was active in promoting the Sequoyah Weavers, a group of artisans whose looms produce some of the finest woolens in the world. He brought industries into the area and initiated the construction of a replica of a Cherokee village for tourists, a pageant on Cherokee history that is played nightly throughout the summer, and a Cherokee restaurant and craft shop, all in the old Cherokee capital of Tahlequah in Oklahoma.

He counsels continually that Indians should work hard to maintain a positive image, pointing out that Indians cannot win friends by force and that militancy damages constructive causes.

President Lyndon Johnson appointed Mr. Keeler a member of the National Advisory Committee for the War on Poverty Program and to the President's Committee on Economic Opportunity. Walter Hickel, when governor of Alaska, appointed him chairman of a task force to find ways to improve utilization of native labor in that state, and he was named by the Secretary of the Interior to head a group for the development of plans for reorganizing the Bureau of Indian Affairs. He also headed a task force to study the operations of the Bureau in Alaska and to study native land rights, educational needs, and other conditions. And, he was chairman of the United States delegation to the Inter-American Conference at Quito, Ecuador, in 1964.

Mr. Keeler, himself, advocated that the Cherokees should elect their chiefs rather than having someone chosen for them, a practice that had been in effect with the establishment of Oklahoma statehood and the absorption of the tribes living in Indian Territory. He encouraged the passage of the legislation that changed this situation and threw the office open to election. When the election was held, even though Indians of greater degree of Indian blood ran for the office, it was Keeler all the way, so great had been his sympathies and his efforts for his Cherokee people.

When he was notified that he was to stay on as Principal Chief, Mr. Keeler said that he would continue to develop human resources among the tribe and to build up profitable businesses for them. Also, that he would continue to seek compensation for Cherokee lands not previously paid for and to contest the ownership of the Arkansas River bed. Decisions have to be made concerning a judgment of $4.2 million awarded the tribe through settlement of a land claim, and work will begin on a constitution, probably patterned after the one for which John Ross was the major architect and which put the executive power in the hands of the chief and the legislative power in an upper and lower house.

In the past five years a beneficial impact due to Mr. Keeler's activities has been felt by 17,000 Cherokee families. He is determined that those Cherokees still on welfare rolls shall be removed and restored to a self-sustaining life.

"There has been too much emphasis," he maintains, "on custodial responsibilities and too little on the development of the people to take over for themselves."

William Keeler has not only devoted himself to the Cherokees in specific and to Indians in broader areas, he has given of his time and talents to numerous professional, educational, civic, and governmental organizations. In 1971, his contributions to his state, his nation, and his industry were recognized with the bestowal upon him of the Outstanding Oklahoma Oil Man Award, the highest honor of the Oklahoma oil industry.

Mr. Keeler carries his many honors modestly. It is his philosophy that the reward is in the doing and in the accomplishment and, like the Cherokee leaders of old, he remains one of "the people"—working with them, not for them, reaching out for their benefit, not reaching down for their patronization.

For some time, Indians have been traveling a downward

path, Mr. Keeler reminds us. Unfavorable conditions which were totally beyond his control have left deep scars, the result of government actions of the past and present, or public misunderstanding.

In almost every Indian community there are distress situations, he points out. There are broken people, apathetic people, those in ill health and unhappiness in great magnitude. To these conditions, there is no simple solution. "Government and others can probably do no more than insure us equal opportunity. The rest is up to us individually."

Mr. Keeler makes these suggestions to his people: "Forgive the past and remove resentment from your hearts. Even the strongest person cannot carry such a burden for long. The Creator gives each man his talents. We must be true to ourselves. Laying aside our talents and going in search of others is to throw away our native strengths. Let us hold on to those we have and choose wisely what we add or acquire."

The Indian values were a lack of acquisitiveness beyond one's needs, a deference to others, contemplation without press of time, and a belief that all things were given to man by the Great Spirit, Mr. Keeler says.

"These values could save civilization from self-destruction or make the 'kingdom' come." Indians must hold on to their values, he sincerely believes, for they are the foundation for peace of mind and are a contribution without price to the world.

Peter MacDonald

ONE of the newer Indian leaders who has come to the fore on the national Indian scene is Peter MacDonald, chairman of the Navajo Tribal Council. For years, the Navajos have chosen to remain aloof from Indian organizations, programs, and politics unless they were directly concerned as a tribe. With the election of Peter MacDonald as chairman in 1970, this has changed.

MacDonald, a handsome man of considerable charm, made this clear when he spoke at the annual convention of the National Congress of American Indians after his election.

"The Navajos are as interested in other Indians as they are in themselves," he said. "To achieve new goals . . . we need leadership. We need resources. We need a determination to act in concert as Indians, rather than as isolated members of various tribal groups."

The applause resounded throughout the assembly hall, for the Navajos are the largest tribe and theirs is the largest reservation in the country. Their sovereignty is guaranteed by a United States treaty.

When elected to the tribal chairmanship, MacDonald was the first college graduate to hold this office. He took over a tribal government with an estimated $200 million in assets and more than $67 million in cash deposits and investments.

The Navajo reservation lies in four states—largely in Arizona and New Mexico, and with small areas in Utah and Colorado. Peter was born in a remote part of the Arizona lands in 1928. His father died when he was two, and from then on, it was a constant struggle for survival, not only on the economic level but spiritually as well.

Because there was so little money, he dropped out of grade school when he was fifteen, a sad and mixed-up boy. There seemed to be no hope for him and, coming from a traditionalist home, he was constantly torn with the conflict of trying to reconcile two cultures. He was plagued with feelings of inferiority and entirely lacking in self-confidence.

Peter enlisted in the Marines for service in World War II. He would be paid and he would be fed and clothed, and he would see some excitement.

He became one of the famous Navajo "code talkers," a unit that was one of the best kept secrets of the war. The exploits of this group of volunteer Navajo recruits will go down in history as one of the most vital and colorful contributions of any group of people. The Navajo "code talkers" were top secret throughout the war and for a number of years after it. Through them, the American forces had the only foolproof, unbreakable code in the history of warfare, for the Navajo language could not be understood or translated by the enemy and completely baffled them. The Navajo Marines were able to transmit the most important of messages without any fear of deciphering.

Peter MacDonald served in the Pacific Campaign at Guam and later in China. After the war, with the help of GI money, he enrolled in an electrician's course. But with only a sixth-grade education, the course was too difficult and he was embarrassed over his educational deficiencies.

Twenty years old, he entered a government school and then transferred to a church-sponsored school in Oklahoma. He earned his high school diploma within a year. When his GI money ran out, he worked at odd jobs so that he could continue his education through junior college at Bacone, Oklahoma.

He still had his problems with inferiority feelings, however, and he set about to overcome these, knowing that he would be handicapped all of his life unless he did so.

"I studied about the Dark Ages in college," Peter says, "and I learned that these people of the white race had been just as uneducated, uncivilized, and savage as any primitive Indians. They did not have a superior culture then, so why should they look down upon others when they had their own shortcomings to overcome." Through such reasoning, he overcame his negative reactions to his Indian background.

In 1954, the Navajo tribe set up a $10 million fund to provide scholarships, and Peter was one of the first to qualify. He received his degree in electrical engineering from the University of Oklahoma and for six years was a project engineer on a Polaris missile guidance system at Hughes Aircraft in California.

But the call of home was strong and when he was asked to return and become executive director of the Office of Navajo Economic Opportunity, he cast aside his $18,000-a-year job with Hughes and went back to a much lesser income.

"I have never regretted this decision," MacDonald says. "I needed to achieve that success which only comes with applying your talents for the benefit of those less fortunate. To me, and to Indian people, success is not money. It is not position. It is education and awareness so that you see and recognize the means to develop your character and enrich this by serving other than your narrow self-interest."

As head of the Navajo OEO, he spoke to many Indian high school students, urging them to a commitment to education and leadership. He stressed the awakening of self-sufficiency that had taken place in the tribe within a few years.

"The self-reliance of the Navajos is asserting itself at the grass roots," he pointed out. "It started with hope and it has led to achievement. It will continue to strengthen itself until the day comes when life will be good again for all Navajos. Our young people can best prepare themselves for leadership and success by remaining in school and getting a broad well-rounded education. So commit yourself to this ideal. Your people need you."

Shortly after his election to the tribal chairmanship, Mac-Donald was invited to deliver the keynote address at the third annual convention of the National Indian Education Association. He re-echoed these sentiments.

"It would be difficult indeed to think of another single facet of a person's life as important as the education he receives—not just in an academic sense but in the total sense of everything that comes into play in fashioning him into the kind of person he is."

Peter MacDonald began to make great impact with the thoughts he was expressing, and with his forthrightness of speech—never condemning, but laying it on the line, nevertheless. He was named as a "Distinguished Alumnus" by his junior college. He received the Citizenship Award of the

Sons of the American Revolution, and the Distinguished American Award presented by the National Institute for Cooperative and Economic Development.

The SAR Award was given after he became Tribal Council chairman, and at the same time he was cited by the California Senate's Rules Committee for his many accomplishments and his successful efforts in overcoming adversity.

In one of his first speeches after his election as the tribal head, Peter MacDonald had this to say: "I propose that we build a strategy around our strength. We are physically dispersed, and in the past this has worked against us. Now it can work for us. Our ablest and brightest young people have been relocated to the cities. In the past that has depleted our strength. Now we can turn it to our advantage. In the past the truth has been our greatest weapon but we have never been able to use it to make an effective appeal to the conscience of this nation. Now, we can move to do so. We can use our youth, our geographic dispersion, and above all, the truth, to create a new style of Indian fighting."

Mention Peter MacDonald's name to the Navajos and faces light up with approving smiles. "He is our own child who has gone away to get an education and returned to help our people," they say. "He has worked his way to where he is today and he has become one of the outstanding Indian leaders of the country."

Maria Montoya Martinez

MARIA MARTINEZ stands unique among her own people, and among other people as well. There are few who have accomplished so much or have devoted themselves so exclusively to helping others. Her whole life has been one of creativity in artistic and humanitarian ways.

There are nineteen Indian pueblos in New Mexico, and Maria was born at one of the most northern—San Ildefonso, not far from Santa Fe. The year of her birth was 1887. The Indian pueblos have been strongholds of Indian tradition even to current times, and Maria's home was no exception. Her family was a traditional one, and like the other girls of the community, she grew up in a conservative pattern. She was taught household tasks by her mother, and she dressed in the style of her people, as she does today. She attended and took part in the seasonal ceremonies, and attended a government school for Indians. She married a boy from her pueblo when schooling was over.

Some time before her marriage, Maria was taken on a visit to Spanish-American friends in the old town of Chimayo. There she saw and admired a painted chest, handmade by a member of the family many years before. When she married Julian Martinez, the chest was sent to her as a wedding present and Julian knelt before it in admiration. He wished that he could paint like that. Like all the Pueblo Indian people, the young couple loved beauty and artistry.

San Ildefonso was a farming community and the crops were the main source of income, but a slender one. The Pueblo Indians, for hundreds of years, had been agriculturists. They could raise corn where it seemed no corn would ever grow, and they also raised melons, beans, and pumpkins.

Unlike some other Indian tribes, the Pueblo men were the farmers. The women made pottery and baskets and excelled in these crafts. Every Pueblo girl learned to make the pottery bowls which were used for food and water storage and also sold to tourists.

But store-bought pots and pails began to replace the pottery ones which required much work, and the pottery was beginning to disappear or was of inferior quality. There was not enough market for the handmade bowls to spend much time at them. Desert lands do not produce a large yield from the standpoint of revenue, either. San Ildefonso was a poor community.

Maria and Julian moved to Santa Fe where Julian found employment as a janitor at the New Mexico State Museum. This was a very different way of life and Maria often found herself with little to do. Her house was small, and although the babies soon came, Indian children are raised with little fuss and do not require constant attention.

So Maria began to visit the Museum and to wander among the exhibits. There were many interesting things to see, but most fascinating of all were the beautiful, large bowls—ancient vessels of such fine craftsmanship and intricate design as Maria had never seen. They stirred her emotionally, for they came from a Pueblo past. She began to think seriously about them and then she talked about the pottery to Julian, and then with one of the Museum curators.

This man encouraged Maria to try to reproduce some of the ancient designs in the pottery that she made for sale. He also showed her some shards of a highly polished black ware of which the Pueblos had no knowledge, but which had been found in Pueblo ruins.

Maria's imagination was fired. "I want to find out how this pottery is made," she told Julian. "If I can find out how to make this pottery, it will be something that will belong only to San Ildefonso. Surely the 'ancient ones' will help me to find the secret when they know that I do not ask for myself but for our people."

Julian nodded soberly. He could see how much this meant to Maria. He said he would help her.

And so Maria set to work. She experimented with clays, and with firing, and with slips, the coating that is put on pottery before firing, but never did her pottery take on the black polish of the old pieces. She tried again and again and again. Often the dishes stood in the sink while Maria wrestled with her problem, or kept working, thinking she was about to succeed. And, just as often, she failed and became so discouraged that she thought of casting the whole project aside.

But Julian would not let her. "Keep on," he said. "The secret will be found. A few dishes don't matter."

The experiments went on for years—and then it happened. On one tremendous day, Maria discovered at last that it was the method of firing that produced the satiny black finish of the old pottery shards. But there was still disappointment, for any decoration that was applied vanished when the pottery was fired.

Again Maria became a scientific researcher. Again, with long hours of patient effort, she finally produced a fluid that came out of the firing like dull etching against the lustre of the pottery. She had given much of herself but it had not been in vain.

Now Maria set about to produce pottery in the new method. "It is so beautiful," she told Julian, "that every piece must be perfect. I must improve my own work so that it is worthy of the effort and the result. Truly, the 'ancient ones' helped me and now I must express my thanks."

Maria and Julian returned to San Ildefonso and opened their own studio. Every piece was as fine as Maria's hands could make it. The shapes were symmetrical and in complete balance. She spent hours polishing them with a sheep bone to bring up the high gloss. The pottery was eagerly bought by those who recognized and appreciated the excellent handiwork.

Julian applied the decorative motifs with a brush made from the yucca plant. Now he could give free rein to his desire to paint. No one excelled him in the creation of imaginative birds, animals, and other creatures. A favorite design was the plumed serpent, and also the sun symbol. Some designs were those copied from the Museum exhibits.

When Maria had perfected her skill, she began to teach the other women of the pueblo to make the fine, black pottery. She was a strict teacher, insisting that only quality work could be done and rejecting any piece that was the least bit crude.

Her own pieces were winning many awards and were sought after by museums and private collectors, not only in this country, but abroad. There is some of Maria's pottery in nearly every major art or craft museum.

After three years of successive prize-winning, she refused to accept any more awards. "They are to go to the other women," she said, "so that they, too, will find encouragement and will have an income."

San Ildefonso is the only pueblo which produces the etched black pottery today. The other pueblos respected Maria's right of discovery and have never tried to copy it. An all-black ware is made at Santa Clara, but it is not the same as Maria's and is undecorated. The other pueblos have their own distinctive styles.

Through Maria Martinez an ancient art was restored and developed into an industry which has increased the income of the Pueblo people far beyond that which came from their farm products.

Among the many honors given to Maria were an honorary doctorate from the University of Colorado, an award from the American Institute of Architects, the Jane Addams Award from Rockford College, and an award from the American Ceramic Society.

In 1933, she was invited to exhibit and demonstrate her pottery-making at the Century of Progress Exposition held in Chicago. At this time she was presented the Indian Achievement Award, the second person to receive it. (Dr. Charles Eastman was the first.) Thousands of people witnessed the presentation. Some years later, she received the Palmes Academique of the French Government, presented in special ceremonies in Santa Fe.

Through it all, Maria remained the warm and friendly person that she is. She was undisturbed by the attention and continued on her way, deeply beloved by the people of her village and looked up to by them as a figure deserving great respect.

When Julian died, Maria was too crushed to work for a while. He had been the staff on which she had leaned for encouragement and it was his abiding faith in her that had kept her on her path of creative endeavor.

"He would want me to work, now," she thought. "Julian would not want me to be idle."

When she and Julian worked together, they would autograph each piece of pottery. The autographed pieces, when they can be found, now bring very high prices, as do pieces made by Maria alone—for, as she grew older, she did less and less work.

Her son, Tony Martinez, known by the name Popovi Da, took up the craft and worked with his mother. A popular, active leader, he was several times governor of the pueblo and he opened a new studio to further the pottery-making at San Ildefonso.

Maria turned to research again, and this time developed a new finish that is like a silver overcast on the black lustre.

But then Popovi Da died, and it is problematical whether Maria will continue with the studio. Now in her sunset years, she can look back on a life of outstanding service and of sharing that can never be dimmed. It is as lustrous as her own pottery.

The story of Maria Martinez has been beautifully told in the book, *Maria, the Potter of San Ildefonso,* written by Alice Marriott. It is a fine tribute to this truly great woman.

Billy Mills

It was October 14, 1964. The place was Tokyo. The event was the Olympic Games—the 10,000-meter run.

The audience, tense with excitement as the runners came down the track, saw in the lead a young American Marine. Billy Mills, a Sioux Indian from South Dakota was running against thirty-six of the greatest distance men in the world. If he won the race, he would be the only American to ever win a distance race in the Olympic Games.

During the last 300 yards, Billy was accidentally pushed by one of the runners and he dropped twenty yards behind. Then, in the last 100 yards he pulled up and charged ahead to win. His time, 28:24.4.

It was incredible—unbelievable—the biggest upset in the history of the Olympics, with a new Olympic record established. Billy Mills was suddenly an international hero.

He stood straight as an arrow to receive his Olympic honors, but his manner was one of modesty and dignity—the modesty of a great champion and the dignity of his Sioux people. He was as overawed by what he had done as any person who saw the spectacular run take place.

Billy was a complete unknown in the Olympic world of

sports and he was up against the toughest kind of competition—great track men and popular athletes as well. He had tried for the Olympic team while he was in college and had failed—and now this triumph.

William M. Mills was born on the Pine Ridge Reservation in South Dakota in 1938. His mother died when he was seven, and his father when he was thirteen. His father used to box for a living, but now there was no one to support eight orphaned children—Billy and his seven brothers and sisters.

Billy was sent to a government boarding school. It was a hard time for him and he had to make himself stop feeling sorry for himself.

He attended high school at Haskell Indian School in Kansas, and while there he became interested in sports. His father used to give him pointers about boxing, and so he tried for the boxing team. He also played football, but at this he wasn't too successful.

At first, he wasn't interested in running at all. He looked upon the track men as "sissies," and preferred what he thought were more robust sports. When he tried track, he decided that running was just as robust as anything else, and it certainly demanded rigid training.

When he entered Haskell, he had weighed only 104 pounds and was five feet, two inches tall. Running helped to develop his physical stamina and wind and he turned out to be a "natural." As a sophomore, junior, and senior, he won the state two-mile cross-country championships, and the state mile title as a junior and senior. When he graduated, he was awarded a full athletic scholarship to the University of Kansas.

In college, there were many times when Billy Mills almost called it quits. There was no one really interested in his progress. He was shy and withdrawn and often discouraged. His brothers and sisters were scattered and he seldom heard from anyone at home.

But he set his teeth and decided that it was up to him to make good. He continued to run and as a college junior and senior he was a member of the team which won the National Track championships two years in a row. He was the Big Eight cross-country champion, and ran his first 10,000-meter race to set a conference record of 31 minutes.

In spite of this, Billy did not gain much prominence. It was while he was at Kansas U. that he first tried to make the Olympic team and when he didn't succeed, he decided he'd had enough. He didn't quit school, but he did quit track. Before he graduated, he married a classmate and accepted a commission from the U.S. Marine Corps.

Billy forgot about running. During his last year of track competition, he was continually dropping out of races, always badly defeated.

"I didn't realize it then, but it was because of my attitude," Billy says. "I just didn't want to make the effort. I wasn't interested and because I wasn't, it was impossible for me to win. I blocked myself off from winning." Failing to make the Olympic team had thrown him for a complete loss. He just gave up trying.

Although Billy had forgotten about track and field, a fellow officer in the Marines had not. He prodded him into running again, and Billy won the inter-service 10,000-meter run in Germany in 30:08 and got his mile time down to 4:06.

It was the Marines who sent him to the Olympic trials and to victory. Billy's chances of winning were given at 1,000 to 1 odds, but that didn't matter. He had a chance and made the best of it. Those who watched him on that historic day when he beat those odds were elated. The president of the International Olympic Committee openly stated that in his fifty years of watching the competitions, he had never seen an American respond better to pressure.

When Billy Mills returned to this country from Tokyo, he was the idol of sports fans and young people. Now he ranked with the great Jim Thorpe, the Sac and Fox Indian who was an outstanding football player and winner of all the events in the pentathlon and decathlon in the 1912 Olympic Games held in Sweden. But Thorpe had had to give up his Olympic prizes because at one time in his life he had played professional ball with a small team while he was still in school and was no longer an amateur.

Billy was a greater idol to his own Sioux people than to anyone else, however. An old-time powwow was held to pay tribute to the young man who had gone away like a warrior to win his eagle feathers. Honorary songs and dances from an ancient past were seen and heard again, and gifts were given in the Indian custom.

Among the things that Billy received was a ring made of gold from the Black Hills, the sacred ancestral lands of the Sioux.

"I was told that this was probably the closest I would ever get to the Black Hills gold," he laughs, for the lands had been lost to the Sioux many years ago. "The ring is one of my most cherished possessions, because it is something I can wear and show people that I am proud to be a Sioux. It has much greater meaning for me than the Olympic gold medal, although that is cherished, too."

With the Olympic race behind him, Billy traveled to more than fifty countries, speaking to young people wherever he went. He entered business as an insurance salesman and settled down in San Diego with his family.

In the meantime, he had set another record in the six-mile and he was torn between running, making a living, and filling all of the speaking engagements that he had. He decided to try out for the Olympic 5,000 meters instead of the 10,000 meters, for he hadn't kept up his training.

Since he hadn't been in competition, he had to petition the Olympic committee to be allowed in the final trials for the team. But when he arrived at the trial grounds, he was told that he had filled out the petition incorrectly and had asked only to get into the 10,000-meter race. Billy ran in the 10,000-meter trial but failed to qualify. He was told that he could enter the 5,000-meter but was later refused because there was pressure from other athletes claiming discrimination, and a disturbance would be staged if he was allowed to participate.

The Olympic Committee bowed to this pressure, and Billy was eliminated. On the same day that the race took place, though not as a contestant, he ran the 5,000 in 14:32. The runner who won in the trials and went on to the games in Mexico City finished the race in 14:45.

"I was politicked out of the race," Billy says, "and I let it get me. I quit running again, and I started to sell insurance, missing out on my best years of competition. I was also very bitter."

Then he took himself in hand and said, "A man can change things. A man has a lot to do with deciding his own destiny. I can do one of two things—go through life bickering and complaining about the raw deal I got, or go back into competition to see what I can do. I decided if I wanted to do anything, I had to do it myself. I didn't want to wonder twenty years from now, if I could have done it."

So he began to train again, "not setting any time limit or particular aim. If it doesn't come out right, you're just frustrated. I want to keep a clear mind and get in shape. If I don't make the Olympics, I may go into the 1972-73 indoor season, get some quality races, and then leave the field."

When Louis R. Bruce became Commissioner of Indian Affairs in 1969, he asked Billy to join his staff and visit Indian young people in government schools around the country. Billy understood only too well the depression that Indian youngsters can fall into, and he felt that this was a way he could help them. In his speeches, he says: "Indians quite frequently and to a great degree are their own worst enemy. We expect the government to change things for us and we sit back sometimes and wait for them to do it. I was the same way after I was kept out of the Olympic trials. And I know it is the wrong way to be."

He shows a film of the race that he won, and plays the tape recording of the event. He talks about his life as an Indian and his life in relation to sports.

"My Indianness kept me striving to take first and not settle for less in the last yards of the Olympic race," Billy says. "I thought of how our great chiefs kept on fighting when all of the odds were against them as they were against me. I couldn't let my people down."

He emphasizes over and over that he won because he wanted to win. "I wanted to make a total effort, physically, mentally, and spiritually. Even if I lost, with this effort I believed that I would hold the greatest key to success."

Indians have great athletic ability, Billy states simply. "They have ability far greater than mine, and if they are given the opportunity to explore and develop their talents, they can achieve any personal and educational goal they choose, especially if they make this total, physical, mental, and spiritual effort."

In 1972, Billy Mills was named one of the ten outstanding young men of the country by the United States Junior Chamber of Commerce. He "overcame great odds to distinguish himself as an Olympic athlete, a Marine Corps officer, and as an effective spokesman for his people. His personal success, professional accomplishment, and service to mankind are the products of his drive and determination," his citation reads.

N. Scott Momaday

"INCREDIBLE! I just don't believe it!"

This was the way Scott Momaday greeted the news that his first novel had won the Pulitizer Prize. He had not been aware that the book had been submitted for consideration for the prestigious award.

Dr. Momaday is the son of Natachee Scott Momaday, a Cherokee, and Al Momaday, a Kiowa. His mother has also written a number of books and his father is a well-known artist and teacher.

Scott grew up in the Southwest. His parents, who were employees of the Bureau of Indian Affairs, were stationed on a number of reservations, primarily among the Navajo and Apache, and in the New Mexico pueblos. Scott, however, was born in Oklahoma in 1934.

He went to a number of government schools for Indians in his early years, because his parents were frequently transferred. He was very much at home among Indians, whether of his tribe or not, and he came to have a deep and abiding love for the Southwest country.

"My roots are there," he says. "I have a mighty longing for that landscape and I can't stay away very long. I have to go to Monument Valley on the Navajo reservation for my own peace of mind, to get lost in the loneliness, the magnitude, and the mysticism."

This love of the land, and this "oneness" with it that is typical of Indians, comes to the fore in Scott's writings. His Indian readers find much to appreciate in his description of the landscape and of Indian traditions, but Scott's works appeal to the emotions of others as well.

In his last year of high school, Scott was sent to Virginia Military Academy. A studious youth, his academic record was excellent. When he returned to New Mexico, his parents were stationed at Jemez pueblo. Here, Scott came under the influence of an old Spanish priest who instilled in him a love of poetry that is reflected throughout all of his writings. The mystical attitudes of his Kiowa people, of the Indians of the Southwest, and of the old priest are all blended in writings which are a form of prose poetry.

Scott entered the University of New Mexico for his degree and then taught for a year on the Jicarilla Apache Reservation. It was while he was among the Apaches that he first began to write. He concentrated mainly on poetry, in which he sought to retain the Indian perspective of "looking closely at the landscape severed from the world of technology."

Scott Momaday's poetry brought him a Creative Fellowship at Stanford University where he was to complete studies for his Master's and a Doctorate. He received the Woodrow Wilson Award and the John Hay Whitney Fellowship and with his Ph.D. in hand, he began to teach English at the University of California (Santa Barbara). Later, he went to the Berkeley campus as associate professor of Comparative Literature.

The Pulitzer Prize book, *House Made of Dawn*, was

written sporadically during a three-year period. It is drawn from the author's own experiences while growing up in the Southwest. The story is about a young Indian who returns to the reservation after discharge from service in World War II. He finds he cannot adjust to his home, nor can he adjust to life away from the reservation in a large city.

Abel, the young Indian, is patterned after other Indians Scott knew. His controlled bitterness and violence erupts in a killing and finally in his complete disintegration.

"I was too young to go into service," Scott says, "and I escaped the harsh discrimination that I have heard other Indians speak of. A lot of the boys I knew, though, died violent deaths and there's a lot of violence in the Indian world just now. It's one of the manifestations of a loss of identity. The confrontation between the Indian and the rest of America is essentially violent."

Momaday refers to this as a "psychic dislocation." He thinks that, in the long run, assimilation of the Indian is "inevitable," but he feels that Indians should not be de-Indianized.

"It will be possible, I am sure, for Indians to retain elements of their traditions. Certainly, they have things of great value to give to others . . . his attitude, for example, or way of looking at things," Scott says. "I think the Indian really does have a clearer view of the natural world. He has managed to live on peaceful terms with nature. The rest of the world seems to be destroying itself."

Momaday explains this by saying: "The native vision, the gift of seeing truly, with wonder and delight into the natural world, is informed by a certain attitude of reverence and respect. It is a matter of extrasensory as well as sensory perception. In addition to the eye, it involves the intelligence, the instinct, and the imagination. It is the perception not only of objects and forms but also of essences and ideals.

"The Indian beholds what is there; nothing of a scene is lost upon him. In the intensity of his vision he is wholly in possession of himself and of the world around him. Most Indian people are able to see in these terms. Their view of the world is peculiarly native and distinct, and it determines who and what they are to a great extent. It is indeed the basis by which they identify themselves as individuals and as a race.

"In contrast, most of us in this society are afflicted with a kind of cultural nearsightedness. Our eyes, it may be, have been trained too long upon the superficial, the artificial, aspects of our environment. We do not see beyond the buildings and billboards, the monuments of our civilization, and consequently we fail to see into the nature and meaning of our own humanity."

In respect to such things as a sense of heritage, a vital continuity in terms of origin and destiny, a profound investment of the mind and spirit in the oral traditions of literature, philosophy, and religion, the Indian is perhaps the most culturally secure of anyone in America, Scott Momaday believes.

In his own life, Dr. Momaday has entwined both Indian and white cultures, enriching his association with the white man's world with strong ties to his Indian background. He is easily a part of the academic world and he plans to bring the Indian into his classroom. At Berkeley, he has set up an Indian literature program and hopes that it will attract Indian students. He hopes, too, that other Indians will join the faculty.

"Indians are creative people," he points out. "They express

themselves in artistic, in poetic terms. They are great artists, and now their songs and stories, all with poetic imagery, are gradually finding their way into public acceptance."

Momaday is concerned about preserving Indian folk tales and legends. He says it is vital to do so, and that this must begin at once, because each generation moves further away from the traditions.

"If anything, the generation gap is more pronounced among Indians than in the rest of America," he says. "Stories are handed down from one generation to another as they are remembered. Not one was ever written and they will be lost forever if not collected now."

He wants to encourage Indians to become writers, not only so that traditions and legends will be preserved, but because they can interpret Indian culture and history as no one else can. Indian history, so far, has been one-sided, and the other side should be told, he points out. His literature program is wholly dedicated to the preservation of legends and folk tales and is the finest college course to be so structured.

"I am convinced that American Indian culture has greater sensibility for language than almost any other culture," Dr. Momaday tells his colleagues.

"Our children are being bombarded with television commercials, radio, and the slang propagated by junk mail. As a result, the sensibility for language has been dulled. Yet, because of its isolation, because it is not written, the Indian language is not so vulnerable. It has retained a sense of poetry and an affinity to nature that could be a boon to the young.

"My people, the Kiowa, for example, tell remarkable

stories full of beautiful and intricate plots with great concern for human attitudes and their relation to nature."

It was to his Kiowa people that Scott Momaday returned for his second book, *The Way to Rainy Mountain*. The book retraces the three hundred-year-old migration of the Kiowa from the headwaters of the Yellowstone east to the Black Hills and south to Wichita. The author talked with contemporary members of the tribe, taping interviews and recording the memories of the trek that have come down among the people as real history. The published result is really two books in one. The even-numbered pages are the tribal history and the odd-numbered pages are Scott's own memories. Both have been described as "prose poetry, sensitive, aware, lovely and philosophical."

Some of his earliest memories are of the summers he spent with his Kiowa grandmother and hearing from her the Rainy Mountain story, the history of the Kiowa migration, of the Sun Dance, and of the golden days when the Kiowas were horsemen and feared warriors, moving about over the Plains with honor and glory. The book is illustrated by Scott's father, who also knows well the traditions of his people.

In speaking of the Pulitzer Prize, Dr. Momaday says: "I hope that it is an indication that the Indian is coming into more recognition than he has had previously. I think there is a greater awareness of the problems Indian people face, but not a sufficient awareness. And there is not anywhere near enough awareness of what Indians can do and accomplish. I want to see this recognition that has come to me serve as an incentive and encouragement to Indians to enter the world of writing.

"Writing can be real drudgery. I sometimes think it is a

very lonely sort of work. But when you get into it, it can be exhilarating, tremendously fulfilling and stimulating."

With the winning of the Pulitzer Prize, Dr. Momaday has been deluged with requests for articles and books on aspects of the Indian community. But, although he will keep on writing, he doesn't feel that the award will necessarily mean instant success for any other work. "I don't think I can write a bad book and sell it just because I am a Pulitzer winner," he says.

Barney Old Coyote

A YOUNG Indian boy of the Crows, on his way to high school, heard some stupendous news. While waiting to board the bus, he learned that Pearl Harbor had been attacked! Japanese planes had struck down American ships lying in harbor, and a full-scale war had been launched!

Leaving his books behind him, the boy rushed home, borrowed money, and headed for the recruiting office in Billings, Montana, where he enlisted in the Navy. He was just seventeen.

The boy was Barney Old Coyote, the son and grandson of earlier Old Coyotes, and the great-grandson of Mountain Sheep, a noted chief of the Crows. Barney was born on the Crow Reservation in 1923.

The Crows, originally settled in North Dakota, for a time lived in earth houses and were a farming people. Then they migrated to Montana and became hunters. They obtained horses around that time from herds that had escaped from the Spaniards and wandered onto the northern Plains. The horse changed their entire way of life. The people became buffalo-hunting nomads, wandering between the Rocky Mountains and the prairie, and doing no planting of any kind. Like all the tribes of the area, they lived in skin tipis which they carried with them when on the move.

Living between the powerful Sioux tribes on the east, and the strong and equally hostile Blackfeet on the north, the Crows were constantly under attack and constantly forced to fight to defend their hunting grounds and to survive as a people.

Although they were never a large tribe, they had a proud tradition as warriors. The men wore their hair quite long, and in battle it streamed out behind them like a flag. Crow Indians could always be recognized by this loose and flaunting hair which almost dared the enemy to take their scalps.

Some of the men liked to go about with hair touching the ground and would add to the length of it by braiding in other strands of hair so that it hung to their heels.

A man who led a Crow war party also trimmed his shirt and leggings with hair. When he struck an enemy in battle, the highest of all war honors, he fastened wolf tails to the heels of his moccasins. If he had snatched a bow from an enemy during battle, he decorated his shirt with ermine skins.

The first treaty was made with the Crows in 1825. The Indians pledged their loyalty to the United States and remained loyal from that time. They served as scouts and as couriers in the various Indian wars and skirmishes that took place, and Crow scouts marched with Custer.

It is told among them that when camped, Custer's flag on its standard fell over three times. The Crow scouts took this as a bad omen and advised Custer not to go on. Custer disregarded this and met his fate when he and all of his men were killed by the Sioux camped on the Little Big Horn.

The story of the Custer battle is enacted by the Crows on

their reservation each year. The battleground and memorial monument are only a short distance from the reservation.

Barney's grandfather, Old Coyote, was a scout with General Crook, the commander of Army troops instructed to round up the Sioux and place them on reservations, and his great-grandfather, Big Forehead, was the Crow hero of the Battle of Rainy Butte.

Barney's older brother, Henry, persuaded him to change from the Navy to the Air Force, saying that he would do the same if Barney agreed.

After basic training, the two were on a flight to Africa. The plane on which Barney was a crew member was caught in a hurricane and damaged beyond repair. A forced landing was made in Puerto Rico, and, returning to base, Barney found that he was a man without identity. All of his records had been lost at sea and until new ones arrived, he had to remain where he was.

As soon as he could do so, Barney re-enlisted for overseas duty. His brother was now with a ferry command stationed in Egypt, and he wanted to join him. His mother wrote a special plea to the government which was granted and the two were together again.

The Old Coyote brothers were sent to Tunisia where they fought with the 15th Air Force. When they received their honorable discharges, each had completed fifty missions and each had been decorated many times for courageous action.

Barney is said to be the first Indian ever to fly the Atlantic Ocean. He was the first Indian to shoot down German aircraft in combat, and the first Indian to take part in the destruction of an enemy submarine. His first decoration was presented to him by General Mark Clark of the Fifth Army, who was Commander of all United States forces in the Mediterranean Theatre. It was given for "extraordinary heroism."

When Barney returned home, he was the center of special attention from the Crows, who considered him a hero of heroes. His exploits as a military pilot earned him the right to carry the pipe, a privilege given only to leaders of Crow war parties in the past.

The fact that he volunteered for war duty gave him the right to carry two pipes, and these, encased in beautifully beaded bags, are slung across his horse when he leads Crow processionals.

Barney was also given the right to wear a chief's jacket decorated with fifty white weasel skins. The jacket was given to him by the family of a Sioux chief who had adopted Barney as a son when his oldest son died. It was presented with full ritual by a Pawnee who had survived the Bataan death march.

When Barney put on his complete regalia, many ceremonies were necessary. Honor songs were sung, and he took part in the War Bonnet Dance, relating the brave deeds that earned the people's respect. A "giveaway" feast followed the ceremonies, with many gifts distributed in his honor.

Barney returns regularly to participate in the ceremonies and other events held by his people. He leads the chiefs and head men in all processions. Once he was asked, "How can you leave this—the color, the sound of the drums, the dancing, and return to the city?" He replied, "With a broken heart."

Barney Old Coyote is the prototype of the modern Indian leader—highly successful in his chosen career, but holding the traditions of his people equally important and meaningful.

One of Barney's first acts on his return to Montana was to

complete the test for his high school diploma. Then, wanting to work for and further the interests of Indian young people, he entered Morningside College for his degree. He then held a number of positions with the Bureau of Indian Affairs on western reservations.

Because of his fine record, Barney was picked to be special assistant to Secretary of the Interior Stewart Udall, in charge of the newly developing program, the Job Corps. As coordinator of this project, he was to help young men and women train for useful and productive work.

This he saw as an opportunity to constructively help Indians and other deprived young people. About his work, he said: "One of the basic needs is not for more money, nor for more programs, but for dedication to the underprivileged to help them help themselves through all existing programs and opportunities."

There is no simple solution to poverty, Barney believes, but it is feasible to eliminate the condition. Only the will to do so is lacking, he thinks, saying that there "should be work toward effective government at all levels, and there must be changes in attitudes with new approaches to the whole subject."

Leadership can and should be provided toward a concerted effort for systematic and orderly planning for the development of our national resources, Barney says. "This leadership should extend into redirecting the energies and attitudes of our citizens in a manner that embraces all segments of society."

Barney disagrees with those who say too much has been done for the American Indian, and also with those who feel that "we can never do enough for them."

"Not nearly enough has been done for Indians, who have

a special relationship as the original owners and as citizens that others do not have, but some of it has been misguided or misdirected, or was not adequate to the need. Too much should never be done for any people, for this will destroy and undermine the will to do for one's self."

He also disagrees with those who say that "the Indian will never reach a level that will make him a useful citizen, either to himself or to his nation."

"Too many Indians have proved differently," he points out, "and many more, given the opportunity, will do so."

There have been great men in previous generations, he explains, and today we have a highly sophisticated, developing leadership such as we have never had before. But in the past, what Indians said was usually disregarded and seldom heard beyond the borders of their reservations.

Now, the federal government has made a public commitment to Indians and whatever steps are taken are highly visible. Indians, too, as they plead their cause, are also highly visible. Public attention is focused through the many books that are being written, through articles in the press and other media, and through TV documentaries and newscasts, or interviews, that turn the spotlight on.

"Indians will merit further and further attention if we are not selfish in our attitudes but demonstrate that we seek realistic goals and the equal rights of any other citizen."

Barney was one of those who retired from federal service with the change in administration. Before doing so, he was awarded an honorary doctorate by Montana State University, the first Indian to be so honored.

In his acceptance speech, Barney directed his remarks to rural poverty and laid down a challenge.

"It is essential," he said, "to strive for a perfect work of engineering, but such perfection has little meaning if it does not serve mankind and make this world a better place for people."

He pointed out that rural poverty is the breeding place for urban poverty and urged that poverty problems be fought where they begin, stating that "no single agency nor a single approach will solve the plight of the poor for long."

After leaving Washington, Dr. Old Coyote was a Field Administrator for the Bureau of Indian Affairs. Stationed in Sacramento, he was engaged in public service work, closely associated with the large number of California tribes and their problems.

He now heads the Department of Indian Studies at Montana State University where he is channeling his efforts to bring about the better understanding between Indians and whites that he advocates.

"Indians must help non-Indians understand them, and non-Indians must help Indians to understand them better."

The interpretation of the history and culture of a people is one way to bring about this understanding.

Helen L. Peterson

HELEN PETERSON grew up on the Oglala Sioux Reservation and is considered to be a member of that tribe. Actually, she is a Cheyenne by blood, although she is an enrolled Oglala Sioux.

When she was born in 1915, she was the first grandchild in her immediate family. Sitting at her grandmother's knee, she was steeped in Indian stories and folklore throughout her childhood. But her grandmother often advised her to "read, write, and talk good so you can work among Indians and help them."

This advice she took quite seriously and her work in behalf of Indian people, and of all minorities, has brought her to the highest position held by a woman in the Bureau of Indian Affairs. She is the first woman to be assistant to the Commissioner.

Mrs. Peterson attended public schools before enrolling at Chadron State Teachers College. Teaching would be the best way to help her people, she thought, but for her, the path was to take another course.

Just out of college, her first position was as secretary to the head of the education department of Colorado State

College. In school, she had financed her way by giving piano lessons and by help from her grandmother and from the National Youth Administration work program. That first position was a welcome one.

Working with the education department, her horizons began to broaden and her ability drew her to other fields. For example, she served in Nelson Rockefeller's national office of Inter-American Affairs as director of the Rocky Mountain Council on Inter-American Affairs at the University of Denver Social Science Foundaton.

This was to give her considerable insight into world affairs and into minority group problems. She was asked to set up the Colorado Inter-American Field Service Program which later came under the Extension Division of the University of Colorado.

The western states were becoming aware of the troubles besetting the migrant Mexicans and Helen's position was concerned with Spanish-speaking groups. She organized some twenty Latin-American Community Service Clubs and from this work evolved the Latin-American Education Foundation in Colorado.

In 1949, Mrs. Peterson was sent as an adviser to the United States delegation to the Second Inter-American Indian Conference in Peru. She prepared a resolution on Indian education which was one of the few that the United States delegation put through at that international meeting.

Shortly before going to Peru, Mrs. Peterson had been appointed director of the newly created Mayor's Committee on Human Relations in Denver. She organized the program for the Denver city government. By now, she had an established reputation in the field of minority relations.

When the National Congress of American Indians met in

Denver, Helen attended the sessions. She found herself harking back to what her grandmother had said—"that she must work for Indians." She had gone far afield since then, and she wanted to get back to her own people.

When she made her desires known to the Congress, she was offered a position in the Washington office. In 1953, she was appointed executive director and she helped to raise organization sights to the world at large.

For the first time, Indian delegations began to take part in international conferences. Groups were sent to India and to Puerto Rico and to South America. Helen lectured extensively, served on boards of organizations and foundations, and worked to establish university classes in human—and Indian—relations.

This was a period of great activity for the Congress, and among the projects in which Helen was prominent was the Chicago Conference of Indians held at the University of Chicago in 1961.

This was one of the largest gatherings of Indians ever held, and from the various sessions a statement was drawn up which was presented to President John F. Kennedy as the thinking of Indians on Indian problems and their solution. Out of this meeting came the formation of the National Indian Youth Council, comprised, primarily, of sophisticated and alienated Indian students.

With a change of administration in the National Congress of American Indians, Helen returned to Denver. She was reappointed director of the Denver Commission on Community Relations and also of an organization known as American Indian Development.

In speaking to Indian people, Mrs. Peterson sometimes comments on the fear of extermination which developed with the government press for termination of federal services to Indian reservations. This aroused great consternation among all tribes and was strenuously protested.

There has been a continual effort to have the termination bill, which was reluctantly signed by President Dwight D. Eisenhower, repealed. When President Nixon took office, he assured the tribes that there would be no termination plans in his administration.

"Indian tribes have been threatened with extinction in the past," Mrs. Peterson says, "but the danger of extermination has never been greater than today. It comes more from 'within than without.'"

Mrs. Peterson challenges her audiences to define what an Indian is, and what a tribe is. It is easy to define a tribe, but to say what an Indian is, is more complex, because an Indian can be many things. He can be a biological Indian, because he is born into an Indian family of Indian identity and background. He can be a "partial Indian," because he is of fractionated Indian blood. Some tribes will not recognize individuals as Indian if they are of less than one-half Indian blood, and others set no limit on the degree of blood, carrying the Indian identification down to where it is virtually nonexistent.

Some of the well-known "Indians" of very little blood degree were Will Rogers, the famous and beloved humorist, and Charles Curtis, who was Vice President of the United States under President Herbert Hoover. But both men had strong Indian identification. Rogers was a son of a former governor of the Cherokees and in his family background were recognized tribal leaders. Curtis was raised on an Indian reservation and was a descendant of two Indian chiefs.

Indians who are born off the reservation are not recognized by some tribes as Indian; if they are not included in tribal rolls, they are not entitled to tribal benefits; and if they are "component"—that is, with parents from two different tribes—only one tribe will accept them as Indians.

The government, in its dealings with Indians, has not recognized those below one-quarter Indian blood as entitled to Indian benefits and services. This, it maintains, is only a technicality which makes the rendition of services more feasible.

There are Indians of a large degree of Indian blood who choose to ignore their identity, and there are those of almost no Indian blood who are more Indian in their attitudes and associations than many Indians. There is no law which establishes what is an Indian.

Mrs. Peterson is sharply critical of both older and young Indians who, she says, are "destroying our own community leadership." At the same time, she has faith in those young people who aspire to gain an education in order to strengthen and support Indian leaders.

"Dollars cannot measure the worth and value of your cultural identity," she points out to Indian youth. "Therefore, don't let some of the current fads destroy your tribal association and your Indianness."

One of the fads among certain of the young people is to refrain from any mention of tribal background. They want to be known just as Indians—one people—but tribal identification is necessary where property and other rights enter in. To destroy tribal identity is to destroy protection.

"Indians have a very special relationship with the federal government through the commerce clause in the Constitution, and some 375 treaties, 5,000 laws, and 5,000 regulations," Mrs. Peterson says. They have had legal status as citizens only since 1924, however, although some Indians became citizens before that through special circumstances. Those who volunteered for duty in World War I, for example, were automatically made citizens, and those who married non-Indians, or who gave up tribal rights and property, could become citizens.

The person responsible for the 1924 Indian Citizenship Bill was Charles Curtis who was then Senator from Kansas and the "whip" of the Senate.

"American Indian tribes have their differences, just as nations do," Mrs. Peterson explains to white audiences. "But most tribes have a legal local government which includes executive, legislative, and judicial branches. The United States government reserved land for tribes and acts as trustee of property rights to the tribes because they were here before the federal government was organized.

"Sovereign rights were inherent in the tribes. They were real, and the colonies and the government acknowledged that sovereignty. Only the Congress can diminish tribal sovereignty."

What divides Indians most today, Mrs. Peterson believes, is the lack of understanding of what are the facts and the truth. Those unfamiliar with tribes other than their own tend to believe that what applies to one applies to all, and this is far from being so.

Arthur Raymond

ARTHUR RAYMOND has a number of "firsts" to his credit. He is the first Sioux Indian ever elected to a state legislature. (He was elected to the North Dakota legislature in November, 1971.) He is the first Indian to be elected to the state legislative body. He is also the first working newspaperman ever elected to the North Dakota state legislature.

Arthur has set a record for being "first" in other ways throughout his entire life. He was born at Winner, South Dakota, one of a large family of ten children. His father died when he was nine and his mother when he was fourteen, and he has been on his own since then.

When he was eleven, Art was already at work, for he then had his first steady job. He graduated from grade school at the head of his class and then was sent to the Rosebud Indian school, where he also graduated at the head of his class.

In high school, Art continued his record for scholastic excellence. He was editor of the high school paper, editor of the annual, and a delegate to the first "Boys State" held in South Dakota. He was president of the senior class, president of the student council, co-captain of the football team, and chairman of the adult education program, among other activities.

Journalism attracted his attention before anything else at school, and he intended to pursue this career. But, with the advent of World War II, he enlisted in the Army as a private and worked his way up through the ranks.

By the war's end, he was commander of an infantry company with the rank of First Lieutenant. When he was commissioned a Second Lieutenant, he was among the youngest to hold this rank.

While in the Army, Art served first as a medic, and as such, he attended and was graduated from Surgical Technician's School at the top of his class numbering two hundred individuals. Sent overseas, he served in Europe in the famed 35th Infantry Division. He joined a rifle company as a replacement and it was this company that he commanded when the war was over.

Art then returned to the States. Remaining with the Army, he was battalion and then regimental athletic officer. When his own division was deactivated, he transferred to the Fifth Infantry and was a rifle platoon leader. Thereafter he was promoted to commander of a rifle company of the 10th Regiment in the same division. By then he was ready to leave and he requested inactive duty status.

Returned to civilian life, Art worked briefly as assistant boys' adviser at his old school at Rosebud, then as a physiotherapy assistant at a polio center.

But like the fire horse that responds to a fire alarm, he responded to the call of journalism, his first interest, every time he read a newspaper.

"It was something I had to do," Art says. He enrolled in

Dakota Wesleyan University and buckled down to the hard work of financing his way.

"It was far from easy," Art says, "but then, I had worked hard all my life so I wasn't afraid of it. At one time or another I had been a laborer, a truck driver, an archery instructor—because who knows better how to shoot a bow and arrow than an Indian—a lifeguard, a dairy worker, a cook, a hospital orderly, a janitor, a dishwasher, and a salesman. That's quite a checkered career."

But from all of this background came something of value—an ability to relate to the man on the street, and understanding of human behavior, and an ability to make people real to other people.

In college, he was again editor of the student newspaper and a member of the Student Senate. His editorials in the newspaper won him the top award of Sigma Delta Chi, journalism fraternity, for 1950. He was also named by the *Wall Street Journal* as the outstanding economics student of 1951, based on his writings on this subject as well as on his scholastic record.

For a while Art worked part time for the Mitchell, South Dakota, paper, joining the full-time staff after graduation. He was promoted to city editor that same year.

He gained much recognition throughout the state when his story of a robbery-murder-suicide won the national first prize from the Associated Press as the best story of the year. This same story was selected by the Pulitzer Awards Committee for nomination.

While on the paper, Art was appointed by the governor as a member of the South Dakota delegation to the White House Conference on Youth. He was also given the 4-H Community Service Award for outstanding contributions to his community, for he was active in many civic affairs and served on numerous councils and committees. He was a member of the Episcopal Executive Council for the state, on the board of St. Mary's School for Indian Girls, national president of his university's alumni association, and an officer in the Veterans of Foreign Wars, among other activities.

Art was especially interested in wildlife and recreation and, as president of the area's sportsmen's club, worked for added wildlife and recreation facilities on Missouri River main-stream dams.

It was Art Raymond who conceived and directed the "Mr. Mitchell" program, which paid tribute to a local citizen for community accomplishment and which became an important annual event.

Art was now given the position of managing editor of the Williston, North Dakota, *Herald*. Again, he made himself a part of the community. He was a member of a drill team unit, president of the North Dakota Associated Press, a member of his church's biracial commission. In both South and North Dakota, he was a Sunday school teacher and licensed lay reader for many years.

Throughout his career, he made a study of the Sioux nation and became one of the leading authorities on the history and customs of his tribe. He addressed historical societies and schools throughout the state on this subject and wrote many articles about the Sioux which were published in various newspapers and magazines.

He is also a recognized spokesman for the Sioux and is frequently called upon by his people for special advice or services. He is extremely proud of his heritage, but he says that "heritage will not put food in my stomach or clothing on my back.

"I am convinced that I can do more to help my people by making my mark in life in the free competitive society in America against all comers. The Sioux are in dire need of men and women who can make this kind of mark, for Indians have long had a negative image among those who do not understand them," Art comments.

It isn't necessary for Indians to return to the reservation to be of service to their people, he believes. Those Indians who go into the cities, into the professions, and into the vocations, and achieve success are good will ambassadors for their people and do equally as much to serve their people, because they break down barriers that come about through a lack of communication and a lack of "rubbing elbows."

Indians have so long been removed from the surrounding society, and isolated from the country at large, that this has led to ingrown attitudes and an unwillingness to be a "part of" or to meet others halfway.

Arthur Raymond is convinced that Indians have an obligation as well as a duty to establish themselves as equal citizens and to assert themselves for their own advantage. That nothing is to be gained from backwardness, but everything is to be gained from articulate expression and the broadening effects of experience and "mingling" is his philosophy.

Tests by educators and psychologists prove that the Indian has talent in equal distribution to the general population, he remarks. "He is just as good and just as bad, just as normal and just as abnormal, as his contemporaries. Then why has he remained a victim of his environment?"

"Because I am an Indian, I must act like an Indian," does not apply, Art stresses. "The burden of proof is on the individual, not on the race."

He points out to Indian youth that the ability to exchange

talents, jobs, work, words and ideas—freely, confidently, and intelligently—is one of the accomplishments of human beings. "To do less is to betray your forefathers who survived the law of a primitive world that you might live. To do as much is to prove the Indian race a resurgent force, able to live in the most advanced, the most fiercely competitive, era of mankind. To do more is to pass on to your progeny the noble heritage your forefathers gave you."

When Art became an editor with the Grand Forks *Herald*, he covered the state legislative sessions for a number of terms. His reporting was so excellent that he was persuaded to run for state legislator, and won with ease. In this capacity, he hopes that he can more concretely help the various tribes of the state in legislative or other matters where state and Indian relationships come into play. Indians come under the federal government rather than the local, but there are some situations where the state gets involved in Indian matters. There is a state Commission of Indian Affairs, there are public schools enrolling Indian children, and there are a number of ways in which a state legislator could very effectively improve things for Indian people.

Then, too, with Arthur Raymond's qualities of "to the fore if I can," the legislature can be a stepping stone to Congress, where Indian voices are needed.

Ben Reifel

THE name Ben Reifel is an illustrious one both among Indians and in the halls of Congress. Dr. Reifel has a solid record of enduring contributions to his people, his state, and his country, and a record of personal accomplishment that few have equaled.

Ben was born in a log cabin on the Rosebud Sioux Reservation in South Dakota. The country surrounding the cabin, which was built by his father, was bleak—open to the bitter winter winds and the burning heat of summer. It was hard to wrest a living from such land as this. The Sioux had never been farmers but buffalo hunters, so the state of the land to them had not been important. When they were placed on reservations and told to farm, the poor land nearly defeated them.

From the time he was a little boy, Ben had to help with the work of planting and cultivating the few crops that could be raised and with the care of the cattle and horses. The life of the small farm accustomed him to hard work, strengthened his muscles, and hardened his body.

At night, he would stretch out on the floor and listen to stories from the past when older Indians visited the home.

Ben's mother was a full-blood Sioux from an outstanding family. She had many relatives who could speak of the old days from experience, and Ben learned much of his people's history.

His mother spoke little English and had no schooling, but she was influential in shaping the lives of her children, her son says. "She inspired us to make something of our lives, and to find the way to bridge the gap between the old life and the new."

His grandmother never accepted the white man's ways. She refused to sit at a table and ate all her meals sitting on the earth floor. She slept on the floor, too, and she was often distressed that her grandsons were growing up as "white men" and not Indians.

It wasn't easy for Ben to go to school. The nearest one was some distance from home, and his father did not want him to go. He believed that children were to help with the work and that education was not necessary for reservation life. He wouldn't let his son ride a horse to school, and so the boy walked.

Ben had other ideas. Somehow, he sensed that the older Sioux were living in a dream world of past glories and that younger Indians would not be able to continue in that fashion. There was a larger world outside and he wanted to know about it, to be a part of it.

So, he trudged to school when he could and stayed out when he was needed for the seasonal farm work. He wasn't able to complete eighth grade until he was sixteen. Not once did he ever pity himself, or feel downtrodden or poor. He was glad for the opportunity of any schooling.

His father refused to let Ben go on to high school, so he worked on the farm for three years. But like the old Sioux people, he had dreams of his own. Somewhere he had gotten hold of a book, *Giants of the Republic,* a collection of stories about American heroes—George Washington, Abraham Lincoln, and others. He read the book from cover to cover and over and over until it was in tatters, and he absorbed the stories with all of his emotions. There were no Indians in the book, although there had been Indian heroes, too. While it was not a conscious thought, perhaps the feeling was there that someday his name would be known and that he would make his mark as a leader of the modern Sioux.

The urge to get an education could not be denied, and finally Ben ran away from home to enter high school, 250 miles away. Understanding his son's determination but not in sympathy with it, his father made no attempt to bring him home. Ben was free to go his way.

He was so persistent a student, and of such unusual ability, that he came to attention and friends made it possible for him to enter college. He decided to major in chemistry and dairy science, for he was keenly interested in agricultural improvement. Perhaps those bleak reservation acres could be made to yield better income and this would be a way to help the Indians living out in the hinterlands.

Ben obtained his Master's degree and then was appointed farm agent by the Bureau of Indian Affairs. He was stationed on the Sioux Reservation at Pine Ridge. While he was in college, he had been commissioned a Second Lieutenant in the U.S. Army Reserves. With the outbreak of World War II he was ordered to active duty. He returned to inactive status in the Reserves as a Lieutenant Colonel at the war's end.

For a time he was superintendent of the Fort Berthold Indian Agency and then, still wanting to further his education, he accepted a scholarship to Harvard University where he proceeded to get his Master's in Public Administration. On another scholarship, he continued his work at Harvard to obtain his Doctorate. He was one of the first Indians to receive a Ph.D.

While he remained in the Indian Service, as an organization field agent, Ben helped Indian tribes form business committees under the provisions of the Indian Reorganization Act of 1932. He then became superintendent of the Pine Ridge Agency, the first Indian superintendent in its history. He was also one of the first Indians to become an agency superintendent in the Bureau of Indian Affairs.

Among his people, Reifel thought and talked as straight as a Winchester. He wanted them to know that he was on their side, and he was, but he also wanted them to change from habits and attitudes that would never let them get ahead.

Reservation existence was a timeless one. There were no clocks or calendars to hold people to a schedule, and no one wanted any. It was an aimless sort of life, bound to have a demoralizing effect.

"Indians must recognize what our problems are," Ben counseled. "It is not enough that others are aware and think in terms of solution. It is we who must search for answers before outsiders can give us effective help. Plans that evolve must be Indian plans for which we are willing to struggle at any cost to complete."

In the American way of life, he pointed out, those who move with the social stream are future-oriented. Those whose lives are governed by Indian values are oriented to the present. Indians must become conscious of time, of clocks and calendars, and of saving and of hard work. "We cannot without disastrous consequences disregard any of these elements for long if we wish to have a meaningful part in the America of today," he maintained.

He has also said, "Indians must adapt themselves as the tribes of old did . . . they must turn their backs on the past if they are to succeed and survive."

This was a courageous position to take, for it is never easy to turn away from the beliefs and traditions of one's people, especially where traditionalism is well-entrenched and clung to. This was not a denial on Ben's part of the ways of his people, for he is Indian in his respect for the good in Indian heritage. Rather, it was a farsightedness and an objective view that weighed in the balance what must be discarded and what must be held for that proper blending of old and new that his mother had instilled in him.

Before he left the Indian Service, Reifel was named Area Director for the Aberdeen, South Dakota, office, responsible for the Indian agencies and government Indian schools in North Dakota, South Dakota, and Nebraska. He resigned this position in 1960 to run for Congress from South Dakota as a Republican. He easily defeated two well-known opponents in the primary election and enjoyed a sizable plurality in the final election. In each successive election—he spent five terms in Congress—he was re-elected by larger margins, and he did not run from an Indian district.

Dr. Reifel took the oath of office as a Congressman on January 3, 1960. His feelings, as he thought back over his life and the journey from the humble log cabin to the House of Representatives, were deeply stirred. When he was interviewed as the only Indian in Congress, he spoke of his hopes for the future of his people. He wanted to see industries move near reservations and he wanted better education for Indian youth. Reservations are depressed areas, he said, and "we are obliged as a nation to keep improving the Indians' lot."

"Because I advocate a change in cultural patterns, critics have rebuked me by saying that the Chinese and the Jewish people and other ethnic groups have been able to maintain their cultures, and they question why Indians should lose theirs as they would if they lived like other people.

"But they forget that there is no people in America who have worked harder, or saved more than the Chinese and the Jewish groups. After they made their money, then the Chinese establish their Chinatowns and parade with their dragons. Indians have got to learn that."

He confounds the militants by saying: "Very few of our people are really exercising the advantages available to them under the establishment."

Ben Reifel "chose not to run" for Congress again at the end of his fifth term. In one of his final committee meetings, he heard himself described by his colleagues as one who had always been in the forefront of those who care about people and programs meaningful to the United States.

One Congressman said: "Dr. Reifel has been one of the nation's outstanding members of Congress. It is not only his competence and ability, but his deep and abiding love for humanity which have been daily reflected . . . It is his kind of America which will keep the country from burning."

Ben's integrity had left an indelible mark and he was not to be permitted to leave Washington. He was asked to serve with the National Park District as special assistant for Indian programs, an unsalaried post.

And President Nixon appointed him chairman of the National Capitol Planning Commission, an agency acting both for the city of Washington and for the federal government in District of Columbia planning and in reviewing all major construction projects. Out of his abiding love for America, and for Washington, itself, Dr. Reifel gladly accepted.

Ben Reifel was awarded the Indian Achievement Award when he was first elected to Congress. When he retired from the Indian Service he was given the highest honor of the Department of the Interior, the Distinguished Service Award. When he left Congress, he was presented with a special citation by the Interior Department and an honorary doctorate from the South Dakota college where he received his first degree.

Along the way, there have been other honors, awards, and recognitions, and undoubtedly there will be more to come.

Everett B. Rhoades

Everett Rhoades, a Kiowa and the first Kiowa to win a doctorate degree and complete medical training, was born in Lawton, Oklahoma, on October 24, 1931. His grandmother was a full-blood Indian who married a white physician.

Everett grew up in the small country town of Meers in Oklahoma. Although he identified with the white side of his family, he also identified with the Kiowa, and very strongly. He studied Kiowa history, was familiar with the cultural patterns, and greatly admired his Indian people. When it was his time to marry, he married into the tribe. His wife is a full-blood Kiowa.

Physically, Dr. Rhoades is not a "recognizable Indian." When people call this to attention, saying in surprise, "You don't look like an Indian," he shrugs. "What is an Indian supposed to look like?" he asks. "Do I have to look like an Indian to feel like one?"

Feel like one he does, so much so that he is a member of the Kiowa Tribal Council, serving on its land management committee. He took a prominent role in the writing of the tribal constitution, and in securing passage by Congress of

169

a bill which authorized the disbursement of tribal judgment funds awarded by the Indian Claims Commission. He was also active in a number of land transactions that benefited the tribe.

In high school, Rhoades was a good athlete, excelling in baseball and basketball. With a physician in his family background, it was natural for him to be interested in medicine and to choose medicine as a career.

He entered Lafayette College, the only Indian recipient of a scholarship awarded by Zeta Psi fraternity. There, he was a member of the student council and was elected to Phi Beta Kappa.

To enter medical school at the University of Oklahoma, he applied for and obtained a John Hay Whitney Opportunity Fellowship. Part of his education was also financed through a Department of the Interior Indian scholarship loan and grant.

In medical school, he was a distinguished student. He was elected to Alpha Omega Alpha, an honorary medical scholastic fraternity. He received a Polio Foundation Award and the Student Research Achievement Award.

Dr. Rhoades interned at Gorgas Hospital in the Panama Canal Zone and then returned for Internal Medicine Specialty training, again at the University of Oklahoma. He became Chief Resident in Medicine at the University's medical center and in this period he became interested in infectious diseases.

After he completed his residency, he served five years on active duty in the U.S. Air Force at Lackland Air Force Base. He was Chief of the Infectious Disease Service at the base hospital and while there he was awarded the Air Force

Certificate of Merit and was certified by the American Board of Internal Medicine.

With his honorable discharge from military service, Dr. Rhoades accepted an appointment at the University of Oklahoma Medical Center as Chief of Infectious Diseases at the Veterans Administration Hospital and as Assistant Professor of Medicine and Microbiology. Again he was honored, with his election to Sigma Xi, the honorary scientific fraternity.

Dr. Rhoades still holds the above positions. He has written numerous research papers on the subject of his specialty and has served on many medical boards and committees. At one time, he was consultant to the Surgeon General for his area.

In 1970, he was sent by the American Medical Association and the Agency for International Development on a special assignment to South Vietnam. He was a consultant to the University of Saigon Medical School in six weeks of bedside clinical teaching of medical students. On the return trip to America, Dr. Rhoades delivered lectures at the University of Berlin and in Copenhagen.

Among the basic requirements for well being among all peoples, good health is one of the most desirable, Dr. Rhoades says, like any doctor.

The United States government, in its paternalistic care for Indians has for some time made provision for administering to Indian health needs, he points out. Originally, this was provided by military surgeons, since Indians, at one period, had the status of "prisoners of war."

"At one time, the government agreed to provide vaccination and medical care to the Ottawa and Chippewa Indians, but it exacted an agreement that the Indians would remain on their reservations and would also cede some of their land," he quotes from history.

Because he is an Indian, Dr. Rhoades made an intensive study of the Indian health situation and health problems. He learned that gastroenteritis, otitis media, influenza, and pneumonia were the most important diseases among Indian people. Indians have a higher birth rate than the national average, with the highest percentage of deaths among infants and children. Infant mortality among Indians is twice that for the general population.

There were also racial differences in the nature of illnesses, Dr. Rhoades discovered. Peptic ulcers are much less frequent among Indians than among whites, especially in the Southwest, and most abdominal operations in Indians are for gall bladder disease. Cancer of the stomach and the intestinal tract are the major causes of malignancy, which is not true for Caucasians, he says.

At one time, Dr. Rhoades participated in a research project, conducted by a team from the University of Oklahoma, which was set up as an Indian powwow. A brush arbor, like those used by the Indians, was built in order to encourage Indian participation. The fact that one of the team was an Indian, who took part in the powwow activities and understood the rituals, was also helpful in securing Indian cooperation.

While many of the Indian people were interested, Dr. Rhoades says, they refused any procedures such as blood drawing or X-rays. There was fear of these, and also a fear that a disease would be uncovered which would lead to hospitalization or even to the development of an illness.

One of the great disappointments, Dr. Rhoades comments, was the failure on the part of the Indian leaders to exert any influence on the people. Although the leaders stated their own interest and their willingness to cooperate, they would fail to carry through in talking to the heads of families, or to make announcements to the encampment. Neither did they set the example by taking any of the tests.

This failure of leadership and the reluctance to seize the initiative, Dr. Rhoades contends, limits full utilization of health resources by Indians. Never one to mince words, he does not hesitate to point this out.

The failure of will is a self-destructive process which perpetuates itself, he says. "It is also contagious and is handed down from generation to generation. A change in the cycle can only be brought about gradually by the action and performance of the people themselves."

Dr. Rhoades frequently cites a specific case as an example of his meaning. It occurred while he was consultant to one of the Public Health Service hospitals.

"A young Indian woman was admitted to the hospital," he relates. "She had severe heart failure and high blood pressure to such a degree that her life was in danger. She was given excellent care by competent physicians and her life was saved, but she was still in danger for one reason.

"In her second pregnancy, she still had not seen a doctor for prenatal care and examination. It was not a lack of education, or a lack of information which had interfered, for this woman had been advised in a previous pregnancy of the need for close medical supervision during future pregnancies."

The barrier this woman faced was based upon a more profound and subtle influence, Dr. Rhoades says. It was difficult to overcome because it arose from a deficiency "not commonly discussed in polite society, and which white people dealing with Indians are not permitted to discuss at all."

The woman suffered from a failure of pride, he says. "A failure of self-esteem, of self-expression. Her will to self-help had been allowed to stagnate. This destruction of will and pride was greatly enhanced by the welfare-providing agencies which, though needed and well-intentioned, were detrimental in the long run to many Indians.

"Development of the will cannot be provided from outside," he points out to Indians when he speaks with them. "This has to come from within the individual; it has to be developed by the individual so that there is a respectable self-image."

It is up to the tribes, themselves, Dr. Rhoades believes. He says: "The burden for this woman's state of health rests upon those in the various tribes. There can be no future tribal identity if the tribes fail to recognize their responsibility in this and like matters."

Although Dr. Rhoades has been most active with his Kiowa people, his interest has extended beyond tribal lines to encompass all Indians. He has participated in many national and state seminars concerned with Indian problems where his main purpose has been to direct inquiry of Indians into themselves, and he sometimes does this quite critically.

"I speak rather sharply in order to gain attention," he states. "Granted, this is not the way to become a popular leader, but it hasn't reacted against me. I believe that Indians have much to offer from themselves but are too often preoccupied with the Bureau of Indian Affairs, or with the 'whites,' whom they blame for all of their troubles. This is negative thinking, and I try to turn matters around to a more positive nature."

Dr. Rhoades is a member of the health committee of the National Congress of American Indians, and of a committee on long-range planning for the Indian Health Service. At the last convention of the National Congress of American Indians, he was one of those nominated for the presidency.

Joseph C. Vasquez

I DO not regret being an Indian, for being one gives me an advantage others do not have. First, I am an Indian, and I am also an American, a good American. I was there yesterday. I am here today. I will be here tomorrow, because I am unique. I belong to a minority with seniority."

These are the words of Joseph C. Vasquez, who goes by the name of Lone Eagle, and who is an Apache-Sioux. From his boyhood, he harbored an ambition to fly like the eagles that soared over his home in Colorado, and this is why he was named Lone Eagle. He became an aviator in World War II, serving with honors, but "much water ran under the bridge" before that took place.

When Joe was a year old, his father was sent to prison for killing a man in a fight that he did not seek, but that was forced upon him. When he was released, he returned to his family a bitter, mean, and vengeful man. The boy stayed away from home as much as possible. He was needed, however, to help with the farm chores and so he suffered through many painful experiences.

One day, when he was walking in the mountains with

a friend, he heard a strange noise overhead. It turned out to be an airplane, the first that Joe had ever seen.

His hands trembled, he couldn't move, he could scarcely breathe. The plane was a clumsy World War I model, built of pipes and tubing and seemingly held together with bailing wire. The tiny engine buzzed and sputtered and it crawled along at about sixty miles an hour. But it flew!

"It was the most beautiful thing I had ever seen," Joe recalls. He was lost in visions of himself as the pilot, able to go anywhere he wanted and faster than anyone else. From up that high, he could see beyond the mountains, and he could fly above the eagles that he so admired.

"Right then and there I made a vow," Joe says. "I vowed that someday I would fly an airplane."

Very often Joe stayed with his Apache grandmother, and she told him stories from that tribe. She told about her father who was able to cross the desert and go five days or more without food or water, and "who could talk with God." She had built her cabin on the exact spot where her father had died.

She told Joe, too, about Geronimo, Cochise, and Victorio, all great leaders of the Apaches, and the boy wished that he could have lived in that time.

"I would have united all the tribes under my leadership," he thought. He fought imaginary battles, but when these were over and he walked home, he was confused and bitter. He was only eight years old, but already he was filled with suspicions about the white man. It was the white man who had brought so many bad things to the Indians.

One day he told his mother that he had made a vow to fly a plane, but he wondered if he ever could because he was an Indian.

"Don't give up hope," his mother said. "If you made the vow, then someday you will. Too many Indians destroy themselves because they give up hope. Just know that you will do it."

It was not long after this that Joe's mother told him he would have to go to work to help support the family. There was no money in the house. He was sent to a sugar beet farm about twenty miles away where he carried water to the laborers in the fields. He returned home to go to school, but each summer he was farmed out in different jobs. This continued until he was thirteen.

When Joe graduated from grade school, the Great Depression was on. It hurt people all over the country, and Indians were among the hardest hit of all. Joe went to high school when he could, but when he was able to find any work, he had to take it. Finally, he quit school and decided to leave home. He left with a bag full of old clothes, his mother's blessing, and a few dollars that his father managed to spare. He was fourteen years old.

Joe went to the nearest railroad, where he walked the tracks until he came to a railroad yard. A group of hobos, or tramps, were gathered around the freight cars and one of them told Joe that there was work to be had on the dairy farms in Canada.

The freight train pulled out after dark, and the man boosted Joe onto a boxcar and he squirmed into a corner. He fell asleep listening to the click of the rails beneath him. Later, the man shook him awake so that they could avoid the police in the next railroad yard. They walked around the yard and got onto the train again when it pulled out.

Eventually, Joe got to Canada, but he had picked up an

education in how to ride freights, how to get on and off, and how to keep from being arrested. He got work on a dairy farm and stayed there all summer, but then hit the road again, this time on a train carrying coal. The stench, the fumes, and the flying cinders were almost unbearable.

Another hobo friend from this train helped him again. He took Joe to a hobo camp when they next got off and taught him the rules of camp life.

Men were constantly coming and going, and at night Joe huddled around the fire with them and listened to their talk. There were frequent hot debates between those who professed to be Communists and those who were not. The Communists added to Joe's feelings that he would get nowhere because he was an Indian, and there was no one to tell him differently.

Joe now began to travel from camp to camp. When he got into a new town he would get some day-old bread at a bakery, and beg for some scraps of meat. Then he would try to get work. He would sweep out stores, chop firewood, clear off snow. The best-paying jobs were those with the railroad as day laborers, but usually a hundred or more men would show up for these.

It was soon obvious that the men who were picked first were all whites, and favorites of the foreman, because they paid him a little money out of their earnings. When all the favorites were chosen, the foreman looked over the rest. Joe found himself one of a group of Negroes, Orientals, and Mexicans—all turned down.

The blood rushed to his head in anger. "I can work as hard as anyone else," he yelled. "We ought to get some axes and bust this yard up."

But he was hushed by the rest, because the ever-present police were armed and they would quickly quell any trouble-makers, and not gently.

One time, in Oklahoma, Joe was riding on a coal train with ten other men. He piled some coal around him to protect himself from the wind, but was aroused from sleep by shouting and the sound of clubbing. The "bulls" had hidden in the engine, and when the train was going too fast for the men to jump, they had appeared and began to beat the hobos with their clubs.

Joe ran from his hiding place and jumped to the next car with the "bulls" after him. It was pitch dark and the train was running at full speed as he leaped from one car to another. He couldn't see the ground, but he climbed down a ladder and let go. The train was on a hill and in the fall Joe was badly cut up and bruised, but had no broken bones. He did have an even more bitter spirit, however, and was more firmly convinced that there were no good white men.

One day, Joe passed through Fort Collins, Colorado, and there he saw a sign reading: "Fly on an airplane. One ride for $2.00."

He had $2.15 in his pocket, and that was all. But it took him only a second to plunk down the money for his fifteen-minute ride, the most wonderful thing that had come his way.

Moving on when the ride was over, he stayed with the trains, but all the time thought about flying. On one of his last trips, he boarded a train in Texas that was headed for Chicago. While asleep, he was shut into a refrigerator car and the door was sealed from the outside. It was impossible for him to escape, and he hadn't eaten for nearly a day. There were barrels of pickles in the car. He broke one open and munched on these, and he exercised to try to keep warm. His hands and feet began to freeze, his teeth chattered, and in sheer panic he banged against the door and screamed for help.

Mercifully, Joe passed out and when he came to, he was in the county hospital in Chicago. He had been in the car for two days.

Joe found his first steady job in El Paso, Texas, after this. For the first time in three years he wrote home to tell of his good luck. He worked for a bakery cleaning up the shop at night and greasing the pots and pans the first thing in the morning to start the new day. He earned $5.00 a week and all the bread he could eat. And he got a side job selling bananas from door to door. With time to himself in the day-time, he entered high school. He sent home money when he could, and he opened a bank account. He got another side job repairing radios, but at the back of his head was still the "flying dream" and it had to be fulfilled.

Writing to an aviation school in Los Angeles, Joe was accepted. Going by train, he realized that this was the first time in his life that he had ever bought a train ticket. It was an exhilarating trip for the "ex-hobo." He was determined that he would become the best mechanic and the best flier ever turned out by the school, which also offered a course leading to a pilot's license.

The tuition fee used up all of Joe's savings, so he worked at his rooming house for free room and board. He did the dishes, made the beds, shopped for food, and made lunches for the other boarders. He was so fascinated with the school that he hated to leave at night but stayed until very late, tinkering with carburetors and electric systems.

On weekends he got his chance to fly, and he had dreamed

of this so long, and read so much on the subject, that he was able to take over the controls on his first flight, to his instructor's amazement. He flew as if he had flown all his life.

He had kept the vow he had made as a little Indian boy of seven. He graduated in the top 10 per cent of his class. He had the reputation of being the best mechanic in the class and the "hottest" pilot in town. But, although he applied at every aircraft corporation in Los Angeles, he was always turned down. "It's because I am an Indian," he thought. "The same old story."

At one interview, all of the frustration and despair broke into the open. He leaped over a desk and grabbed the interviewer by the shirt.

"You won't hire me because I'm an Indian," he shrieked. "Admit it. You don't want me because I'm an Indian."

In his rage, he almost strangled the man, and it took three other employees to pull him off. The police were sent for, but Joe ran back to his rooming house and locked himself inside. He had been out of work for two months and everyone with whom he had graduated had a job. He sobbed to himself over and over, "They just won't give me a job. They won't give me a chance!"

Embittered almost beyond endurance, Joe took a job as a carpenter at the Los Angeles Indian Center. The Center located a job for him as mechanic at an aircraft firm in San Diego. Hardly daring to hope, Joe went there with almost no money, and to his delight heard the words, "You're hired!"

He hitchhiked his way back to El Paso, borrowed two dollars for a license from the father of the girl he wanted to marry, and hitchhiked back to San Diego to begin work.

Exceedingly able, Joe worked his way up from assistant mechanic to crew chief before long. But to him, even more important, was the fact that he was flying every day. It was his responsibility to flight-test new planes that came off the assembly line, locate the "bugs," and give instructions to the crew for their elimination. It was the most important job he had ever had, and it helped to ease some of the bitter feelings.

As a foreman, though, he often ran into difficulties with workers who resented him. As usual, Joe attributed this to his Indian blood. But gradually, as his own attitudes mellowed, he learned that this was not always the case, but was due to a person's individual reactions to "authority." Instead of losing his temper and reacting from his own problems, he began to find a way to work out personnel difficulties.

In 1943, Joe enlisted in the Air Force for war duty. He had a pilot's license and he knew, "backwards and forwards," every type of plane that flew. He was told that he could expect a commission.

When he was sent overseas a year later, the commission still had not come. He was a member of a crew of C-47s and was assigned to a plane because he was such an excellent pilot. Nor did the commission ever come, even when the war was over, though he was well qualified to receive it.

"What I went through in the Pacific was the most taxing, nerve-wracking flying I had ever experienced. Some trips were from Burma to China, which meant flying through the Himalaya Mountains—going between mountain peaks with just a few feet of clearance for either wing. There were many landings in deep fog by instruments alone, and I saw many planes go down."

But in the air, there were no Indians or whites or other races for Joe. These things meant nothing, he said. "I was still angry, but I wasn't as hateful and vengeful as I would have been a few years earlier. Even not getting a commission didn't make that much difference. I had served my country and served it well, and I was happy to be going home. And, even if I was an Indian, I had been wanted and needed."

After the war, the aircraft industry began to open up. There was no longer a policy of "white only," Joe says, and he found a new job with the Hughes Aircraft Company in Los Angeles. Through this job, he was able to enter the aerospace industry at its beginning. Jet planes were the "newest" and the "hottest" and he was soon working on them and flying them. Responsibilities and salary steadily increased and schooling continued in order to keep abreast of the advances in radar, electronics, and jet propulsion.

After twenty-three years with Hughes, Joe became the small business administrator for the company, dealing with the smaller companies that supply Hughes.

Living in Los Angeles, he became one of the most active members of the Los Angeles Indian Center. In 1959, he was elected president of the Center, the leader of 58,000 Indians who are residents of the area.

And now he heard Indian young people saying to him the things he had once said.

"You can't tell me anything," he said to those who complained of discrimination. "You should have walked in my moccasins a few years back. If they hold you down just because you're an Indian, then they are the ones who are no good. Remember—blind hatred can destroy you. I know from experience that when you let yourself get bitter, you are no better than the guy you are bitter against. Pretty soon, you'll become what you hate."

So effective was Mr. Vasquez' work at the Center that he

was named Los Angeles City Human Relations Commissioner. He had given much time to civic activities and at one time was Scout Master of a troop of mentally retarded boys. He is presently a member of the National Council on Indian Opportunity, and is in charge of the Indian Desk, Office of Minority Business Enterprise, in Washington.

"The Red Man will find his place in society," Joe Vasquez says. "Though we know that the way is difficult, it is in our blood to proceed with dignity, no matter what the consequences might be. We must prove to the world that we are people with a purpose."

Annie Dodge Wauneka

I n December, 1964, the first Presidential Medal of Freedom Awards, initiated by President Kennedy shortly before his death, were presented by President Lyndon B. Johnson.

When the name Annie Dodge Wauneka was called, a tall, stately, striking woman stepped forward. She was dressed in the traditional Navajo clothing of printed skirt, velveteen blouse, silver and turquoise jewelry, her hair gathered at the back of her head in a knot.

All eyes were upon this unusually handsome woman. The Medal of Freedom Award is the highest civil honor presented to individuals in peacetime. Only those who have made outstanding contributions to the security of the nation, to world peace, or to cultural endeavor are eligible for consideration. Mrs. Wauneka was one of twenty-one Americans to be so recognized, and the first Indian to be so honored.

Annie was born on the Navajo reservation, the daughter of one of the Navajo's great leaders, Henry Chee Dodge. He was the first chairman of the Tribal Council, holding that office for a total of more than eight years.

As soon as Annie could run and walk about, she helped

to herd her father's sheep, as was the custom among her people. Her father owned large numbers of sheep, goats, cattle, and horses, but the sheep and goats were her favorites. She always had a pet lamb or two and she cared for them with loving kindness.

When she was eight years old, her father sent her to the government boarding school for Indians at Fort Defiance, Arizona. While she was in first grade, the dreadful flu epidemic of World War I struck and many Navajo people died from it. Many of the children at Fort Defiance became very ill and had to be sent home, and large numbers never returned.

Annie escaped with a mild attack. The one, overworked nurse at the school showed her how to clean the kerosene lanterns every morning so that they could be placed in the hospital halls and rooms. The little girl did all that she could to help, and the experience remains with her today as a vivid memory. It was probably the spark that ignited her tremendous interest in Navajo health.

In the spring, Annie had to leave school to return home and help with the lambing. Although she always returned, she missed many weeks of schooling. A further handicap was an epidemic of trachoma, a contagious infection of the eyelid, which struck at Fort Defiance when she was in fourth grade. Because she had not caught the disease, Annie was sent to a mission school until the epidemic was over. When she returned, Fort Defiance had been made into an official trachoma treatment center.

When she had completed fifth grade, her father sent her to school in Albuquerque. It was her first train ride, and excitement was added to the trip when the train was jammed by another and the children going to school had to be taken off. Annie sat by the piled-up luggage all night with nothing to eat until the tracks were cleared and another train completed the trip to Albuquerque. Another child might have been badly disturbed and shaken, but Annie remained calm and collected and waited patiently for the morning to come.

Albuquerque was a much larger school than Fort Defiance, but Annie made friends quickly. For the first time, she discovered that there were other Indians than Navajos, and among her closest chums were the Pueblo girls. She learned to speak English easily and this was necessary, not only to understand her teachers, but because Indians from various tribes could not talk together in their own differing tongues. She tried various athletic activities, too, but the only one at which she was really competent was tennis.

When Annie was thirteen, her father was named chairman of the newly formed Tribal Council. Soon after, he visited Albuquerque Indian School, bringing a number of other Navajo leaders with him. When he spoke to the children in the assembly hall, Annie listened very carefully. She heard him stress the need for an education and how it would help Indians, and she grew up to become a champion of education and its special importance to the Navajos because of what her father said. She was very proud of her father that day, but she was careful not to show her pride because this was not considered correct in Indian society.

Annie completed her schooling at the eleventh grade. But this did not end her education. She continued to learn throughout her life in every way that she could, and especially from her father. She was eighteen years old, and she picked up her former activities of herding the sheep and goats and tending the livestock on her father's ranch. When she was married to George Wauneka, her father sent the young couple to his other ranch at Tanner Springs. This was an entirely different environment than the one in which she was raised and she had to make new friendships with the Navajos in that area. But she and her husband settled down to learn the business of successful cattle ranching.

Annie worked closely with her father in his duties as Tribal Chairman. She attended many meetings where he made speeches, and she heard the long discussions that he held with his councilmen on various problems. She came to understand the troubles that beset her people, and the reasons for their extreme poverty.

When the Navajos were ordered to reduce their stock by the government because of land erosion, the anger of the people rose almost to the point of violence. The livestock, especially the sheep and goats, were a way of life to the Navajo. They were an economic necessity and none could understand why they must sacrifice their animals.

Annie says now that it was the most delicate and the most disastrous situation that the Navajos had faced since their removal and virtual imprisonment at Fort Sumner in 1863-1867. She often heard her father talk about the reasons for and against the program, but he "always spoke with great wisdom and intelligence, and always with the interests of his people in mind."

Chee Dodge often began his speeches with comments on the hardships the tribe had endured at Fort Sumner and on the return home, and he always emphasized that this suffering had been caused by a lack of education. He tried to impress upon his people, over and over, that education was the key to their future.

When Annie went with her father to these meetings she was at first very shy. But he encouraged her to speak, and soon she was speaking remarkably well. "Do not be afraid to speak your mind," her father said, "but never lose your respect for your elders or for the old people who have lived before you. If it were not for them and their courage, you would not be here."

Chee Dodge was also very strict with his daughter. He insisted that she concentrate on the exact meanings of words and expressions so that she could interpret true meanings to Navajos and non-Navajos alike. He had been one of the first Navajo interpreters, and she saw how his deep understanding had earned him the respect of all. After council meetings, her father would often talk with her about what had taken place, and they would discuss the arguments that had been presented.

Annie and her husband continued to manage the ranch, but more and more her father gave her projects and responsibilities that had to do with the people. He trusted her completely, and she began to see how one works for an ideal, and learned about politics. Her father was an astute politician.

Although she had always been close to him, she became even more so during the last days of his life. Shortly before he died, he said to her: "Do not let my straight rope fall to the ground. If you discover it dropping, quickly pick it up and hold it aloft."

After her father's death, Annie set about to hold the straight rope aloft. She worked for her council chapter and continued to act as interpreter. When she was elected secretary, one of her tasks was to interpret for Navajos who were in hospitals. In four years, she was elected to the Tribal Council, the first woman member of that body. She won her place over two men, one of them her own husband.

Annie was appointed to the Council's Health and Welfare Committee as chairman. When the surgeon general of the United States organized the Advisory Committee on Indian Health, Mrs. Wauneka was invited to become a member.

Now she really became a health crusader. First, she concentrated all of her energies on tuberculosis, the scourge of the Navajo. She visited hospitals and talked with the patients, and she visited homes to which patients had been returned as "arrested cases." She visited homes, too, to persuade patients who had run away from the hospital to return and continue with their care. She met with hostility and resentment, and often clashed swords with the medicine men of the tribe. But she made an impact wherever she went, and no distance was too far for her to go.

She taught and encouraged better health habits, advised the people to improve their home conditions, and influenced the Tribal Council to set aside funds for a home improvement program.

"Dirt floors must become a thing of the past," she said. "Sanitation must be improved; there must be a good and adequate water supply, and there must be running water in the homes."

Some Navajos had to haul water in metal drums for a long distance, and it was not always of the best quality. In the desert area, water was scarce and much of the illness could be traced to the water supply. This became one of Annie's major concerns, and she campaigned so hard that a bill was finally enacted authorizing the Public Health Service to construct, improve, and extend sanitary facilities for the Indians. Later, the Tribal Council provided the funds for those Navajos who wanted to follow the "off-the-dirt-floor" health provision.

This was a tremendous victory. With other legislature and additional financial help, many new homes were built on the reservation—neat, compact houses with bright roofs and wooden floors, and small outhouses a proper distance away. Often a hogan stands nearby for the traditionalists who prefer to live in the old way, or for sacred ceremonies.

In addition to her continual movement about the reservation in her health activities, Mrs. Wauneka also had her own radio program, broadcasting in the tribal language health information and guidance. All that she did produced results, for the incidence of tuberculosis was so greatly lessened among the Navajos that it is no longer a major concern. Not in a hundred years has there been so much improvement in the general health of the Navajos as there has been in the twenty years of Mrs. Wauneka's activities. More and more Navajos are seeking medical and hospital care, and the medicine men work also with the doctors as respected partners because Mrs. Wauneka was able to win them to her cause by speaking to them in a language they understood and relating it to the need that existed, and to influence the doctors to appreciate and understand the significance of the medicine man in Navajo life.

Although she had not consciously sought such recognition, Mrs. Wauneka became known throughout the country for her health work. She was honored by the Western Tuberculosis Association for her efforts to free her people from illness. She was named Arizona's Woman of Achievement by the Arizona Press Women's Association. She received the Josephine B. Hughes Memorial Award for promoting the health and welfare of her people, and of the country as a whole, and she received the Indian Achievement Award for her great humanitarian services, among many other honors.

Never afraid to express her opinions, no matter how un-popular they might be, Mrs. Wauneka turned to other con-ditions. She spoke against the use of alcohol, pointing out that families suffered when parents indulged in drink, and that money was going to city courts and to liquor dealers that could better be used in the home.

She was concerned over the infant death rate, far too high among the people, and advocated that mothers should go to the hospital to give birth. She again persuaded the Tribal Council to set aside funds, this time for layettes for newborn babies who more often than not would be wrapped only in a strip of blanket.

She was appointed to the governor of New Mexico's Com-mittee on the Aging and to many other health committees. She attended a meeting on Indian health problems in Alaska, and went many times to conferences in Washington. She was able to start a reservation eye-ear-dental care program.

Like her father before her, she stressed the need for education, and this was only secondary to her interest in Navajo health.

She now well understood the loneliness of the child away at school, but she is convinced that parents must cooperate in providing schooling for their children. She also says that Indian people must be more directly involved in the school-ing of their children.

"Indian parents must have a say in where schools are to be located," she advises. "Children should be allowed to remain closer to their homes, and their parents should have a close connection with their schools."

Nothing is wrong with the Navajos except the inadequate education, she states firmly. "We are a half-century behind the rest of the country. We want to keep our children near us, not send them miles away to a school where we cannot supervise them, but until we can, we must accept the education that we have, for it is the answer to our problems."

"Indian schools must be Indian community centers as well," is her plea.

Six times a grandmother and now in her late fifties, Mrs. Wauneka could, without criticism, turn to a more quiet life. She has reared nine children—but she has no intention of retiring. Instead, she works with the Tribal Council on the Advisory Committee, reviewing and recommending matters that are to come up in Council meetings.

In 1960, a new 75-bed hospital was opened on the reservation at Shiprock, New Mexico—one of a number that were completed or planned. Mrs. Wauneka was an honored guest, and heard herself introduced with these words of the chief of the U.S. Public Health Service:

"No one individual has done more than Annie Dodge Wauneka to foster a wide understanding of health among the Indian people. No one has encouraged them more to take an active part in the health services."

And Annie smiled her beaming smile and replied: "Over the years, I learned that one failure—or even a half-dozen failures—should never be the end of trying. I must always try and try again, and I will continue to try as long as there is breath to do so."

Index

195

THE AUTHOR

MARION E. GRIDLEY has devoted a lifetime to study and work with American Indians. She has been closely associated and identified with Indian affairs since her girlhood and is the author of twenty published books on Indian subjects. She is the originator of the Indian Achievement Award, presented annually to an Indian individual for accomplishment and humanitarian service, and since 1952 has published *The Amerindian,* a bimonthly periodical devoted to Indians on the current scene, Indian history and personalities. In 1970, she was cited by President Richard M. Nixon for her services to Indians through this publication.

She is an adopted member of two tribes, the Omaha and Winnebago, and was given the name of "Little Moonbeam" by the Omaha and "Glory of the Morning" by the Winnebago. In 1965, Miss Gridley received the Woman of the Year Award of the Illinois Woman's Press Association, and her books have received a number of state and national awards. She lives in Chicago.